701

TH

RUTH SEARLE began her c
and although her love of nui
she went on to fulfil her di
biologist. She completed her PhD on humpback whale
behaviour and is continuing with field research that takes
her around the world. She is a course writer and tutor and
has several current writing projects, including a marine
biology textbook and books about the humpback whale.
She is passionate about studying and has almost completed
a second degree based on Earth sciences, cosmology and
particle physics. Her triumphs and struggles to find and
ive her own personal dreams provided the inspiration for
The Thinking Person's Guide to Happiness.

Overcoming Common Problems Series

Selected titles
A full list of titles is available from Sheldon Press,
36 Causton Street, London SW1P 4ST, and on our website at
www.sheldonpress.co.uk

Assertiveness: Step by Step
Dr Windy Dryden and Daniel Constantinou

Breaking Free
Carolyn Ainscough and Kay Toon

Calm Down
Paul Hauck

Cataract: What You Need to Know
Mark Watts

Cider Vinegar
Margaret Hills

Comfort for Depression
Janet Horwood

Confidence Works
Gladeana McMahon

Coping Successfully with Pain
Neville Shone

Coping Successfully with Panic Attacks
Shirley Trickett

Coping Successfully with Period Problems
Mary-Claire Mason

Coping Successfully with Prostate Cancer
Dr Tom Smith

Coping Successfully with Ulcerative Colitis
Peter Cartwright

Coping Successfully with Your Hiatus Hernia
Dr Tom Smith

Coping Successfully with Your Irritable Bowel
Rosemary Nicol

Coping with Alopecia
Dr Nigel Hunt and Dr Sue McHale

Coping with Anxiety and Depression
Shirley Trickett

Coping with Blushing
Dr Robert Edelmann

Coping with Bowel Cancer
Dr Tom Smith

Coping with Brain Injury
Maggie Rich

Coping with Candida
Shirley Trickett

Coping with Chemotherapy
Dr Terry Priestman

Coping with Childhood Allergies
Jill Eckersley

Coping with Childhood Asthma
Jill Eckersley

Coping with Chronic Fatigue
Trudie Chalder

Coping with Coeliac Disease
Karen Brody

Coping with Cystitis
Caroline Clayton

Coping with Depression and Elation
Patrick McKeon

Coping with Down's Syndrome
Fiona Marshall

Coping with Dyspraxia
Jill Eckersley

Coping with Eating Disorders and Body Image
Christine Craggs-Hinton

Coping with Eczema
Dr Robert Youngson

Coping with Endometriosis
Jo Mears

Coping with Epilepsy
Fiona Marshall and
Dr Pamela Crawford

Coping with Fibroids
Mary-Claire Mason

Coping with Gout
Christine Craggs-Hinton

Coping with Heartburn and Reflux
Dr Tom Smith

Coping with Incontinence
Dr Joan Gomez

Coping with Long-Term Illness
Barbara Baker

Coping with Macular Degeneration
Dr Patricia Gilbert

Coping with the Menopause
Janet Horwood

Overcoming Common Problems Series

Overcoming Common Problems Series

Overcoming Common Problems

The Thinking Person's Guide to Happiness

Ruth Searle

sheldon**PRESS**

First published in Great Britain in 2007

Sheldon Press
36 Causton Street
London SW1P 4ST

Copyright © Ruth Searle 2007

British Library Cataloguing-in-Publication Data

A catalogue record for this book is available from the British Library

ISBN-13: 978–0–85969–998–3
ISBN-10: 0–85969–998–6

1 3 5 7 9 10 8 6 4 2

Typeset by Deltatype Limited, Birkenhead, Merseyside
Printed in Great Britain by Ashford Colour Press

To my wonderful mum,
Elizabeth Matthews:

I love you, Mum!

Contents

Preface

This book is about finding the freedom to live the life that you want to live. It's about discovering exactly what it is you want from your life and putting together a plan for achieving it using a powerful new approach called *neuropsychology*.

By studying the science of the brain and mind, I completely changed my perspective on the way we use our minds, the nature of consciousness and of reality itself, giving me an understanding of how to make my mind work *for* me rather than against me. I found new priorities in life and the courage to make the changes that I needed to make.

Life is too precious and far too short to muddle through, achieving less than we know we are capable of and settling for less than we deserve. This book, I hope, will help you to identify your true desires for your life, realize your heartfelt dreams, and enable you to put together a plan for achieving them using the power of your mind and brain.

The Thinking Person's Guide to Happiness is about changing your life from this moment on. I believe in looking to the future. We can of course gain invaluable insights by understanding the past and unravelling some of our problems, but you can change your life *now* without having to go through years of psychotherapy or analysis of the past. By understanding how your brain thinks, you can devise a unique plan – a plan that will empower you to move forward with your life and find your true path.

Human beings are capable of the most incredible achievements. They have put man on the moon, produced the most exquisite works of art, discovered quantum particles; the list goes on and on . . . yet all these achievements began with just a thought and an all-consuming dream.

I hope within these pages you too will discover your dreams and your passion, just as I have. Your dreams and aspirations are special and unique to you. Dare to reach up to the heights of achievement and you could find yourself living the most amazing life that you could only barely begin to imagine, even in your wildest dreams.

Acknowledgements

With grateful thanks to my lovely sister Abigail Phillips for her enthusiasm and patient editing of the first draft of this book, and to my mum and sisters, Hilary and Rachel, for their encouragement. Thanks to my enduring friends Nikki Mitchell and Kay Eagles for their invaluable comments on the early script and to Alison Elson for her enthusiasm and lifelong friendship. Thanks to Bob Tanner at International Scripts for believing in me and helping me to fulfil a dream, and to Fiona Marshall at Sheldon Press for all her help and encouragement. Thanks also for the hard work of Linda Crosby in the editing department, and of the Sheldon Desk Editorial and Production teams. Grateful thanks to Mike Butters for his help with the final drafts, his valuable suggestions and for all his love and support. And finally, thanks to everyone who has inspired my life's journey as well as those who have challenged me and made me stronger.

Introduction: the science of the mind

Despite astonishing advances in the workings of the brain and nervous system, we still have a very shaky understanding of how the brain engenders the mind. Questions about the mind are extremely perplexing and have occupied people since Aristotle's time. Aristotle was of the opinion that the mind was a combination of the functions of the head, the heart and even the blood.

During the Middle Ages, the mind was thought to be a tiny person inside the head of a human called a homunculus. The notion of a 'soul' has complicated the issue considerably, and has generally been outside the realm of scientific investigation. It is only since the late 1980s that questions about the nature of consciousness have been addressed by neuroscience. Prior to this, the study of the nervous system concentrated on the anatomy and physiology of animals, addressing questions such as how signals from the outside world are collected by sensory organs (eyes, ears, touch receptors, etc.) and subsequently processed in the brain, and how movements of the body are elicited by the nervous system. It is this area of investigation that has brought such enormous advances in our understanding of the physical brain.

What we know about the neuron and its connections has been learned in a very short time. In the 1930s, the first studies on the interaction between neurons and other cells were carried out. But it was after the Second World War that the electrical properties of neurons became accessible as a result of electronic equipment originally developed for military purposes. With the advent of the electron microscope during the 1960s, the detailed structure of the neuron could be studied. During the 1970s, it became possible to make electrical recordings from single neurons using anaesthetized animals without invading the skull. By the 1980s, it became possible to study the molecular channels in the cell membrane that regulate the electrical properties and behaviour of the neuron, but it is only recently that scientists have been able to study the activities of the living brain with sophisticated scanning equipment.

It may be too soon to expect an answer to the far-reaching questions we have about the nature of the mind and of consciousness. Indeed, far from answering these questions, studies of physiology, psychology and other specialties have identified more questions than answers. This is not a failing by any means, but an illustration of how our scientific investigation progressively asks deeper questions about the world we live in. It also says much about the human psyche. We are not content with simple explanations, but are curious to achieve an ever-deeper understanding and strive to answer the hard questions such as 'What is consciousness?'

Modern science has amalgamated many areas of study with the realization that the brain and mind are intrinsically interconnected, and names such as 'cognitive neuroscience' and 'behavioural neurobiology' are used to describe these areas. The most successful area of study into the functioning of the brain during the past century has been that of neurons and their interactions with one another. However, given the complexities of the brain, its functioning cannot be predicted from its smallest constituents, the neurons, even in the simplest animal brain. There are many unanswered questions remaining about how a collection of neurons in the brain can trigger complex behavioural responses.

As well as philosophy, psychology and neuroscience, consciousness has also been the subject of study within the diverse fields of mathematics and physics. Since physics is concerned with the study of natural laws, what it has to say about consciousness is no less valid than any other discipline. Its concern for the basic nature of matter within the universe could have important consequences for our understanding of the nature of consciousness. The hard question concerning consciousness is how the subjectivity of consciousness can interact with the physical brain. Physicists argue that the subatomic particles of quantum mechanics are the key to understanding consciousness as a 'state' of matter. The nature of consciousness appears to be a mysterious 'extra' dimension to the physical functioning of the brain, however complex this turns out to be. One thing seems clear, though. An explanation of the mind, or consciousness, must ultimately be an explanation of the way that neurons function, since there is nothing else on which to base a scientific explanation.

With an understanding of how our brains work (given the confines of modern science to date) we can use that knowledge to make our mind work for us rather than against us in order to achieve the success in life that we aspire to. We can appeal directly to our subconscious, bypassing the complex construction of psychological barriers and past conditioning that has built up over our lifetime. We can delve deep into our psyche to discover the dreams we have for our lives without undergoing years of psychoanalysis.

If we can understand how our brains 'think', we can make our minds work for us now.

1

About the brain

The evolution and development of the brain

The brain has evolved alongside other organs, systems and tissues of the body, and is a product of natural selection. There are adaptive advantages in having a nervous system to co-ordinate the functions of a large animal, although it is by no means the only way of co-ordinating distant parts of a living organism. Plants achieve complex organization without a nervous system by means of physical and chemical signals. Even in complex animals such as humans, co-ordination can be achieved using hormonal and other chemical signals sent via the bloodstream. For example, the immune system is activated by chemical signals between blood cells, while the endocrine system operates via the secretion of hormones within specialist glands. The immune system can take several days to clear an infection; hormones take a few seconds to reach their target organs.

The advantage of the nervous system is the phenomenal speed at which it operates; a nerve impulse in the leg can travel at 200 m.p.h., although even at this speed there is a lag of about half a second between the brain receiving the stimulus, creating a mental representation of it, and then reacting to it. This half-second delay while the brain processes the stimulus is called *preconscious processing* and, as the name suggests, we are not consciously aware of a stimulus for that half-second. For example, if you step on a sharp pin, you are not consciously aware of it for half a second while the brain is processing the stimulus from the nerve endings in your foot. In an animal, the advantages of a speedy signalling system to ensure rapid reactions (such as drawing away from danger and escaping from predators) is vital, and so the nervous system has evolved as a mechanism to ensure survival.

In vertebrates (animals with backbones) the embryo folds in upon itself during the first few days of development to form a tube called the neural tube, which runs along the midline of the back. This tube pinches off from the outside surface and becomes the spinal cord. The brain is formed at the upper end of the neural tube by further

1

folding and development. The spinal cord is practically a self-contained organ enabling an animal to move about. The limb muscles are controlled by bundles of neurons leading off from the spinal cord and can be activated wholly from the spinal cord itself. Mostly, though, it is the brain that is involved in co-ordinating voluntary movements since they are influenced by a complex array of other signals from the sensory organs – sight and hearing for example.

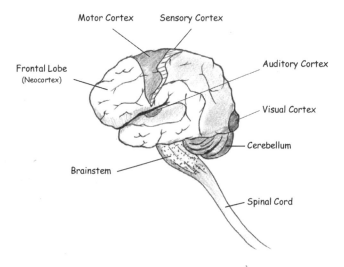

Figure 1 Gross structure of the brain viewed from the side
The main areas of the cortex are shown, along with the other visible structures: the cerebellum and the brainstem. The cerebellum is involved with movement and co-ordination. The brainstem consists of the midbrain, pons and medulla, which are responsible for survival functions such as heart rate, blood pressure, respiration and sleep. It is sometimes referred to as the 'reptilian brain' since it is the oldest in evolutionary terms.

The brain itself (see Figures 1 and 2) weighs approximately 1,400 grams, looks like a lump of porridge, and has the consistency of blancmange! It consists of two halves that are linked together by a bundle of a billion or so neurons forming a structure called the corpus callosum. Signals from the sensory organs (except the sense of smell from the nose) cross over to the opposite side of the brain, so that a signal from the right eye, for example, will cross over to the visual cortex of the left hemisphere of the brain for further processing. Modern scanning methods (described in the next section) have allowed scientists to map the areas of the brain responsible for different functions. In addition to studies of the anatomy of the brain, there is now the possibility of understanding the functions of the brain by studying the genes responsible for the development of the nervous system. This may help us to understand how a collection of neurons is able to function as a whole brain.

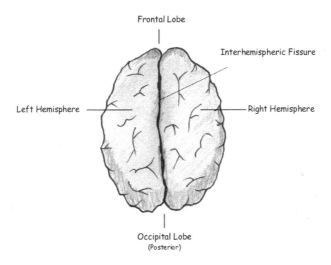

Figure 2 The two hemispheres of the brain viewed from above
They are joined by a tough bundle of nerve fibres called the corpus callosum.

Mapping the brain

There are various ways of studying the brain, ranging from single cells to whole brain organization. Sophisticated neuroimaging techniques have revolutionized neurophysiological research and have given neuroscientists the opportunity to study the whole living brain.

Single cells
Cells can be studied under powerful microscopes and their electrical activity recorded using fine electrodes. This technique is widely used in animal studies, but rarely in humans.

3

Electroencephalogram (EEG)

Using electrodes attached to the scalp, the changes in electrical potential in the brain are measured. These electrical changes arise from the combined activity of many cells in the underlying area of the brain. Electrical activity was first measured in 1875, but the first EEG was used in 1929 to record simple resting alpha rhythms of the brain. By the 1930s the EEG was routinely used in neurology, and by the 1960s computers allowed more advanced studies of the brain. The EEG is still used today, although more sophisticated techniques are used to study the living brain.

Event related potential (ERP)

An event related potential is a tiny signal embedded within an ongoing EEG. It reflects neural activity related to sensory, motor or cognitive events over time and is obtained by averaging out a person's EEG traces. ERPs have proved useful in diagnosing disturbances in neurological activity, such as those seen in multiple sclerosis and hearing problems.

Magnetoencephalography (MEG)

Related to ERP, magnetoencephalography measures magnetic signals given off from active neurons and can locate the source of the activity in a particular region of the brain more accurately than ERP. The main problem with MEG is the prohibitive cost of the equipment used, and its relatively limited use in neurosurgery.

X-ray computed tomography (CT)

CT scans were developed in the early 1970s and are computer generated images of tissue density. X-rays are passed through the body at various angles and measured by a computer as they travel through various tissues in the body. The mathematical methods of constructing the images resulting from CT scans are used in the more modern methods of scanning, and two-dimensional images in the form of slices of brain can be obtained. CT scans are useful for studying lesions of the brain, such as those caused by a stroke or tumour.

Transcranial magnetic stimulation (TMS)

In TMS or repetitive TMS (rTMS) a coil held over the brain generates a pulsed magnetic field that stimulates neurons in a focused area. When motor areas of the brain are stimulated, involuntary movements occur and this, used in conjunction with scanning, allows motor areas to be accurately mapped. Speech and visual areas can also be mapped since TMS suppresses function in the area stimulated. It can also be used to induce particular experiences.

Positron emission tomography (PET)

PET scans are an invasive method of measuring brain metabolism, glucose consumption and blood flow. A radioactive substance is administered intravenously to the patient in the form of glucose, which then enters the active cells of the brain. The PET scan measures brain activity by studying the uptake of oxygen by the cells and the blood flow travelling to neurons. The radioactive substance emits positrons that are detected by the detectors placed on the head. Brain activity is represented in the form of coloured maps, and has helped researchers understand the neural basis of functions such as speech perception and comprehension, memory, reading, attention and many others. PET has good spatial resolution, which means that it allows researchers to see how the functions are localized in the brain, although the obvious disadvantage is the use of radiation, which limits the number of suitable patients for PET scans.

Magnetic resonance imaging (MRI)

An MRI scanner shows pictures of the structure of the brain in much greater detail than a CT scanner is able to do. It is a non-invasive method, because MRI measures the radio signals emitted by certain atomic nuclei in the brain. When a magnetic field is passed over the head, hydrogen molecules reverberate and can be picked up by the scanner, which converts the activity into an image of the brain. In the 1970s, the idea of using hydrogen atoms in the body for imaging led to advances in mapping the function of the living brain called 'functional magnetic resonance imaging' (fMRI); fMRI and MRI scanners have been used to study language, attention, vision and memory among other functions, and can be used alongside PET scans.

More recently, in 2000, fMRI scanners were used to measure the state of 'being in love'. Researchers wanted to find out if the brain behaves differently when people are in love, and measured brain activity under a variety of different conditions. They found a mixed pattern of brain changes when participants looked at pictures of their lovers, with both visual and emotional parts of the brain being activated. The researchers concluded that there was indeed a specialized system of the brain involved in the experience of 'being in love'.

How your brain thinks

The great advances in human intelligence are the result of the amazing development of the neocortex, the frontal part of the brain responsible for thinking and reasoning. The neocortex (which means 'new brain') in humans contributes an incredible 95.9 per cent of the total cortex (it is around 84 per cent in a dog, to give you a comparison).

Your brain is made up of neurons (see Figure 3), the cells concerned with signalling, as well as other cells with ancillary functions (many we haven't identified yet and that may turn out to be more significant that we realize). One important type of cell in the brain is the 'glial cell' (which gets its name from the Greek word for 'glue'). Glial cells give physical support to neurons and also function as a sort of scaffolding mechanism along which neurons can migrate to their final destination during the development of the brain. Research in 2001 suggested that glial cells may also determine the number of synapses between neurons, with neurons that were exposed to glial cells generating seven times more synapses than those that were not (synapses are important for the formation of neural networks in the brain).

Neurons are the signalling cells, which are the ones we are most interested in. Neurons have different shapes or types according to the area of the nervous system in which they are found. Neurons in the spinal cord, for example, can be several centimetres long, while the neurons in the cerebral cortex are just millimetres long.

The neuron consists of a cell body, or soma, and a number of long projections called neurites, which come in two varieties: dendrites and axons. Dendrites are the tiny tree-like branches of the neuron that form up to 90 per cent of the surface area of the neuron. Each dendrite may be up to 1 mm in length, and they may themselves be covered in tiny dendritic spines on which the synapses are made that connect them to other neurons. The dendrites form the basis of the neural networks that connect neurons to one another in the brain. Each neuronal cell has one axon, which varies in length from a few mm to over a metre, and is surrounded by a protein called myelin, which functions to increase the speed of the signal.

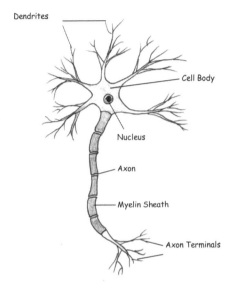

Dendrites

Cell Body

Nucleus

Axon

Myelin Sheath

Axon Terminals

Figure 3 A typical neuron from a mammal

The cell body contains the cell nucleus and other structures essential for the functioning of the cell. The axon and the dendrites carry electrical signals to neighbouring neurons. The myelin sheath covering the axon helps to speed up the signal.

Neurons are extremely sensitive to chemical and electrical energy and there is a small permanent voltage (between one-tenth and one-twentieth of a volt) between the inside and the outside of the neuron. This is achieved via potassium and sodium ions with their respective electrical charges. These ions are able to move across the cell membrane, effectively reducing the electrical charge temporarily for just a fraction of a millisecond at a time. This electrical disturbance, called an action potential, moves very rapidly along the axon like a shock wave. Neurons do not actually touch each other, but are separated by synapses that are just 40 thousandths of a millimetre (a millionth of an inch) across. The signal crosses the synapse via chemicals called neurotransmitters, which are secreted at the end of the neuron sending the signal. When the wave of electrical energy arrives at the end of the neuron, the neurotransmitter is released into the synapse and is absorbed into the end of the connecting neuron. This causes another wave of electrical disturbance to move through the connecting neuron. All this happens at lightning speed.

The amazing thing is that from such a simple mechanism of sending signals between neurons, our brain is able to construct the sophisticated and very complex images and thoughts that we experience constantly. Part of the explanation is that there are so many neurons in the brain and that they form such a complex network of interconnections. In the human brain there are around 300–500 billion neurons; in fact, there are more neurons in a single human brain than there are stars in the known universe. Each neuron may be able to signal as many as 10,000 other neurons in the same instant. This is just the capability of each neuron – imagine what the whole brain can do!

How your brain feels

A part of the brain called the amygdala is responsible for the recognition and expression of emotion, and is involved in organizing behavioural responses to emotions such as fear or anger. It is located in the temporal lobe of the brain and is part of the limbic system, an ancient part of the brain in evolutionary terms. The amygdala is the focal point between the sensory system, which collects information from the environment, and the subsequent emotional responses.

All emotional responses are composed of autonomic, hormonal and behavioural elements. The autonomic and hormonal elements prepare the body for a behavioural response such as an increase in heart rate and blood pressure in preparation for an angry exchange with an opponent. Our emotional responses can be modified by experience; for instance, we can quickly learn to respond to a dangerous situation by experiencing fear. A conditioned emotional response can be produced when a neutral stimulus is paired with a stimulus that produces emotion. This is often the basis of the various erroneous beliefs that we have, and that interfere with our achievement of success in life – in other words, when the emotions we feel in connection with a situation are simply *conditioned* responses, not our *real* responses to the events we are experiencing.

The right hemisphere of the brain is better at recognizing and perceiving different emotions than the left hemisphere, which is better at experiencing emotions. Neuroimaging scans have illustrated this asymmetry in the right and left sides of the brain. Scans have also shown that the left side of the amygdala is active during the experience of positive emotions. The frontal cortex is also involved with the expression of emotion and communicates with the amygdala. It may be responsible for the regulation of behaviour, which is socially and emotionally appropriate and involves making conscious decisions. The left frontal region of the neocortex may be responsible for the experience of positive emotion, while the right side is responsible for the experience of negative emotion. The electrical and chemical signals triggered in the brain by the experience of emotion also trigger the release of 'neurotransmitters', and an important neurotransmitter for emotion is one called 'dopamine'. When we experience a positive emotion, there is an accompanying increase in the production of dopamine in two of the major pathways in the brain. Dopamine is associated with a feeling of elation, which is why positive emotions produce happiness.

The exact number of emotions that human beings experience is controversial, but the most widely accepted number of basic emotions is six or seven and are as follows: sadness, happiness, surprise, fear, anger, disgust and contempt. Emotions can have beneficial or deleterious effects on our health, and the achievement of success in many areas of our life. Anger has been studied extensively and has been shown to affect the physiology of the body and, like most other negative emotions, is associated with undesirable changes such as an increased heart rate and blood pressure, leading to stress and poor performance. Conversely, studies show that people who are outwardly happy are most likely to have high self-esteem and are content in other areas of their lives.

Emotional states can determine much of our daily lives and are experienced as a response to important events, or memories of those events, and are modulated by our experience. We can even experience emotional responses simply by engaging our *imagination*, and this happens because particular neural pathways have been activated.

It appears that our thoughts, prompted by real or imagined stimuli, evoke emotional responses. The brain cannot distinguish between what is real and vividly imagined. We use our senses to selectively collect information about our environment and our brain interprets it according to our beliefs and experience. We can also vividly imagine something and our brain uses exactly the same neurological connections and associations; in other words, the same neural networks are stimulated. The activation of these neural networks, whether from stimuli in the outside world, or from internal representations, causes a physiological response in the body.

To illustrate this, close your eyes, relax deeply, and remember a happy event in your life. Remember it vividly and really bring it back to life. Put yourself back into that situation and make the image big and bright. Remember the sounds and smells and make them louder and clearer; try to bring everything closer and larger than life. Make sure the image is three-dimensional. Remember the warm happy feelings you had at the time. Now how do you feel? Warm and happy, just as you did back then? Now think of an event when you were frightened. Bring it to life as before, make it more vivid, clearer and much closer. Recall your feelings. Now how do you feel? Just as you did during the event itself?

When you practise these visualizations, you will notice that a visual image can be distant or big and close up, bright or dull, in colour or in black and white. These variations are called submodalities, and if you play around with the images in your mind, you can change the submodalities. Imagine your favourite flower. Make it big and bright and smelling gorgeous. Now make it small, dull and shrivelled up. Play around with the image; change the colour, change the size, the smell and the feel of the flower. You have complete control of these submodalities. This demonstrates that we can control the way we think, and consequently our emotional state. We can use this power to strengthen new neural networks that we are trying to create, and depress any unwanted associations.

Your flexible brain

The brain shows an incredible ability to rewire itself in response to new experiences and learning, even in adults. This ability is called neural plasticity, and it is the network of interconnecting neurons that is the key to learning, memory and behavioural changes.

In the animal kingdom, generally the less complex the brain (basically, the fewer the number of neurons), the more specific and hard-wired the neural connections are and the less capable the animal is of making adaptive (plastic) changes to its environment. If you were to enrich a mouse's environment with a variety of toys and mazes, it would gradually rewire its brain with new neural connections and pathways as it learns to incorporate them into its daily life. The more new things the mouse has to learn, the more new connections it will make. Many experiments have been done that prove this. Imagine the scale of the plasticity and rewiring a human brain is capable of – given that the mouse has a very much smaller brain with several billion fewer neurons than a human brain. The capacity for neural plasticity in the human brain is truly astonishing, and we have the capability to literally take control of our thinking patterns and restructure our physical brain!

There is a major distinction between different types of learning and memory: 'declarative' and 'procedural' memory. There is also a third 'emotional' category of learning.

Declarative memory is a memory for facts such as historical dates, telephone numbers, etc., and is easily learned and easily forgotten.

Procedural memory is a memory for skills such as driving or playing an instrument. It is the 'knowing how' memory, and is a slower process that requires many repetitions in order to improve performance. Eventually, procedural memory becomes second nature and is not easily forgotten – even over a long period of time. Much of our learning requires both factual- and skill-types of memory – such as learning to play the piano – which requires declarative memory for reading music and procedural memory for the finger positions on the keys.

Memory can also be categorized as long- and short-term memory. Short-term memory is temporary, limited in capacity, and is easily disrupted and forgotten. Long-term memory, on the other hand, is long lasting, sometimes over a lifetime, and does not need to be continually repeated in order to retain the memory. Short-term memory can be converted to long-term memory and, as the saying goes, 'repetition is the mother of learning'. Over time, repetition forms permanent new connections in the brain. New neural pathways become permanently entrenched and are stored as memory traces in the brain.

Recent research by Nobel Prize winner Eric Kandel and his associates has identified a molecule called CREB as a key element in turning short-term memory into long-term memory. Short-term memory involves a simple change in the sensitivity of a synapse, which already exists, but long-term memory requires the growth of new synapses between neurons to extend and develop new neural networks. The brain must switch on the genes that make the proteins to build these pathways. It is CREB that triggers the genes into action.

Synaptogenesis is the process of creating new junctions between neurons, thereby extending the neural network. Laboratory experiments have shown how new synapses are formed. When axons are placed close together and stimulated to form new connections, there is an increase in the production of neurotransmitter chemicals (such as GABA, glutamate, Ach and 5-HT), and within hours new receptors begin to form so that production can continue (receptors are built on to the scaffolding of cytoskeletal proteins found on the terminals of axons and dendrites). Within a day or two the density of these receptors is several thousand per square micrometre. While neurotransmitters begin to accumulate in the newly forming synaptic junction, the actual physical structure of the base of the axons and dendrites begins to thicken with the development of new layers of cells ('basal lamina'). Over the next few weeks of development, further changes are seen, with receptor cells increasing in density and maturing into a more permanent form. 'Active zones', as they are called, develop over the course of several weeks. Although a functional synapse is formed very rapidly, following stimulation, it is not an all-or-nothing event. The formation of mature synapses is a protracted process that takes several weeks and relies on repeated stimulation in order to produce the neurotransmitter chemicals that produce these changes. This is why repetition is important when learning something new or establishing a new habit.

Synapses between neurons in the brain begin to form before birth (before 27 weeks' gestation), but do not reach a peak density until after birth (during the first 15 months of life). Synapses begin to form in the deeper, more primitive layers of the brain, and later in the more superficial, cortical layers, associated with thinking and learning. This early synaptogenesis is followed by a process of pruning, called *synapse elimination*, which continues throughout adulthood. Synapse elimination fine-tunes the neural network (see Figure 4) by eliminating the connections that are redundant or have not been strengthened with repeated use. This is why the old adage 'use it or lose it' is true. Neural connections that are not sufficiently stimulated are eliminated, and this may occur because of competition from other neural connections for vital substances in the brain – such as nutrients and chemicals needed for the functioning of neurons.

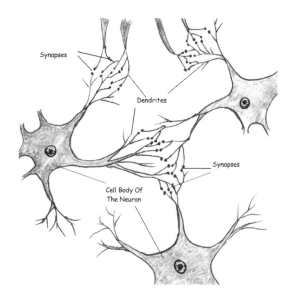

Figure 4 The neural network

When pathways associated with memories or behaviour are created in the brain, dendrites on neighbouring neurons form synapses that pass electrochemical messages along the pathway. Many billions of connections are made and form a neural network in the brain.

As well as creating new networks by the process of synaptogenesis, permanent changes in the brain require continued stimulation of the established neural networks associated with a particular memory or behaviour. *Long-term potentiation (LTP)* is a mechanism whereby existing synapses are strengthened by repeated stimulation of the neurons on either side of it. Donald Hebb proposed this mechanism in 1949 and it is called Hebb's rule. It can be summarized by the aphorism 'what fires together, wires together', meaning that neurons that are repeatedly fired or stimulated form a long-term network of connected neurons. There is also a process linked to LTP called *long-term depression (LTD)*, which reduces the strength of the synapse between neurons. Both work together to enable learning, memory and changes in behaviour to occur.

If you want to learn something so that it is permanently stored in your memory, you need to repeat it. This means not simply repeating it over and over, but reviewing at key times material that is already understood. Tony Buzan, an expert on the potential of the human brain, suggests reviewing material after ten minutes, then the second, third and fourth reviews should follow at increasing intervals, such as a day, a week, a month, and then four months. Memory can be enhanced by using techniques such as mind mapping; creating outlandish stories to emphasize and link facts together; using picture images, associations and so on. The human brain, it seems, has an infinite capacity both for learning and memory by the process of rewiring the neural network.

Human babies have the most incredible ability to learn, and will learn more in the first two years of life than other species of animal learn in their whole lives. Researchers have found that this learning begins even before birth with the formation of memories. As any mother will tell you, her baby prefers her voice to that of anyone else, and experiments have shown that newborn babies suck more vigorously and frequently on a pacifier when they hear their own mother's voice than when they hear another woman's voice. Babies take longer to identify their mother's face though, as there is obviously no way they can know what their mother looks like before birth. But by the age of four weeks, a baby can match its mother's voice to her face, and by 12 weeks it can identify her by sight alone. Another experiment showed that babies form memories before birth, and this was demonstrated when pregnant women were asked to read a story aloud just once a week during the last six weeks of pregnancy. Their newborn babies showed by their behaviour that they preferred this story to any other after birth. The experiment was repeated with songs sung to babies in the womb by their mothers. Again, after birth, the babies preferred the song that they had heard their mother sing. So babies not only recognize sounds, but can remember the finer details of particular sounds such as stories or melodies. It is an evolutionary advantage for babies to bond with their mothers after birth, so it makes sense for a foetus to begin this process before birth. These experiments also showed that babies preferred the language that their mothers speak rather than a foreign language. It is fascinating to realize that children are primed to learn language, whether they are taught it or not, and this, it seems, begins even before birth. Children the world over, whatever language they are brought up with, are self-taught linguists. As long as they are able to hear language, they will instinctively speak and learn the rules of language.

Cognitive development takes place over many years from birth to adulthood, but some functions develop earlier than others. As new neural circuits physically come 'on line', an integrated system of development with perception, reasoning and behaviour progress together as a child's brain grows and builds new neural networks through learning. When we are born, we have a full set of neurons in the brain, and although there is now evidence, contrary to popular belief, that we do grow new neurons in certain regions of the brain during adulthood, the neurons we are born with form the basis of our central nervous system throughout life. However, it is the process of synaptogenesis that enables cognitive and perceptual development to occur during childhood, and results in the extraordinary plasticity in the brain right through to old age. As the neural network becomes ever more intricate with learning, more new synapses are created and the brain matures. This process is evident when a child reaches his developmental milestones.

Using PET scans

PET scans have been used to measure glucose metabolism in various regions of the brain in babies, children and adolescents. One study showed that glucose uptake increases with age in young infants and decreases during the teenage years. In newborns, glucose metabolism is greatest in the deeper structures of the brain and in sensory and motor regions of the cortex, but by the age of two to three months, more glucose is used by the frontal cortex (associated with learning) and in the cerebellum (associated with co-ordination and movement). Glucose metabolism increases in the frontal cortex between six and twelve months, and overall the glucose use in the developing brain increases until about the age of four, plateaus around the age of ten, and decreases gradually to adult levels by about the age of 16 to 18. The older methods of measuring synaptogenesis in the brain (using histological samples) agree with these PET findings.

Another trend in postnatal development is the increase in brain volume during the first six years. This is mainly due to the increase in myelination and the proliferation of glial cells, which collectively form the white matter and function as a support system for the brain. Grey matter is formed from the cortical structures involved with cognition and learning. A study using PET scans on volunteers from ages four to twenty showed that white matter increased consistently with age until adulthood, but grey matter increased prior to adolescence and then decreased. The role of experience and learning on the adult brain was shown in another study when rats living in enriched environments, which foster learning, produce more grey matter in the form of dendrites and synapses – in other words, a more complex neural network than those living in less enriching environments. This proves that even though an explosion of growth is seen in the brain during childhood, throughout life we are able to develop and extend the neural networks in the brain and stimulate synaptogenesis. The plasticity of the adult brain opens up extraordinary opportunities to improve our lives.

2

Consciousness

The study of consciousness

The complex questions concerning consciousness have troubled philosophers for a very long time and we still have no definitive answers. The conceptual issues that arise when we think about the mind are largely subjective ones and are not easily investigated. Traditionally, philosophy has described the mind in terms of what is called *dualism* or *physicalism*, with variations in between.

The French philosopher René Descartes (1596–1650) is probably the most famous dualist. Dualism involves a belief in the existence of a non-physical mind – a distinct substance that is separate from the body. There are a number of criticisms of the dualist philosophy; the most compelling is that it cannot be investigated scientifically.

The more scientifically oriented philosophers of that time, such as Thomas Hobbes (1588–1679), developed a bottom-up approach known as monism or physicalism. Physicalism holds the view that the mind arises from the physical brain and that there is only one substance for mind and body. Physicalists think that if we could look at brain activity in sufficient detail and at all the different levels of organization, then we could understand consciousness itself. One of the criticisms, though, of the physicalist philosophy is that we do not yet know enough about brain processes to prove that the mind arises from the physical processes in the brain, although developments in neuroscience designed to prove this are being made at an astonishing rate.

Consciousness and the question of mind/body, however, are no longer restricted to philosophical discussion. It is now within the realm of neuroscience and the rigours of scientific investigation. Disciplines such as psychology, psychiatry and behavioural therapy appear meaningless without reference to biological processes within the brain. Researchers from a variety of disciplines are turning their attention to the hard questions of consciousness. Frances Crick, famous for his Nobel Prize as co-discoverer of the structure of DNA, has spent the past quarter of a century studying the function of the nervous system, particularly the developing brain in the embryo and

17

the visual cortex with its intimate relationship to consciousness.

Between the two extreme views of dualism and physicalism are many other ideas and hypotheses about the nature of consciousness. The issue of consciousness is about the relationship between brain activity and the subjective experience of consciousness. But however the brain is studied – whether it be to physically dissect it with a scalpel, look at it under a microscope, attach electrodes to it to look at electrical activity, or use any of the modern methods to scan it – the mystery remains: how does this physical lump of biological matter, with all its chemical and electrical activity, function as the seat of consciousness?

What is consciousness and why do we have it?

A simple definition of consciousness is *awareness*. It could be an awareness of a stimulus such as a light or sound or an awareness of the body, of the self, or of the universe. Consciousness is a subjective experience with three basic levels: waking, sleeping and dreaming. There are also other levels of consciousness that could be included – such as lucid dreaming and meditative states.

Many hypotheses have been proposed at every scale of brain functioning from single molecules to large-scale assemblies of neurons, and yet it is still not obvious what we should be looking for. When looking at brain function and consciousness we also have to consider whether the physical brain *causes* consciousness, or consciousness *causes* brain activity, or whether something entirely different causes both. Perhaps brain activity is consciousness.

The current theories of consciousness generally fall into two categories: neurobiological theories and cognitive theories.

The essence of the neurobiological approach is that consciousness arises from the neural activity in the brain, and many researchers are using modern scanning methods such as PET, MRI and fMRI scans to obtain data for their studies. Their ideas all diverge, however, on the areas of brain activity that represent consciousness, and in 1998 there were already over twenty different hypotheses listed for the neural correlates of consciousness.

Cognitive theories describe consciousness in philosophical terms that are more subjective. They are difficult to test scientifically and do not account for the biological aspects of brain function.

Whatever consciousness may be, it has to be an evolutionary

adaptation resulting from the forces of natural selection. All animals (including humans) possess primary consciousness that results in the ability to sense, feel, associate, learn and express emotional states without abstract thinking. This is an adaptive characteristic, which allows us to reflect on a course of action and calculate the benefits and risks of a situation. For example, animals routinely assess the movements of their predators or prey and calculate the most profitable course of action.

This conscious and subconscious awareness is part of our brain and our remote ancestry throughout evolution. In the 1960s, Paul MacLean, a neuroscientist, proposed that all humans possess three parts to our brain: a reptilian brain, a mammalian brain and a human brain.

The reptilian and mammalian brain recapitulates our remote evolutionary history. Indeed, if we look at the structure of the brain, the reptilian part is a simple structure at the top of the spine deep inside the brain and pre-dates the development of emotion. The mammalian part is more sophisticated and is linked to other parts of the brain. It is the part that developed alongside emotions.

The final part is the human brain, which is the *neocortex* or 'new brain'. This is the outer layer of the brain and the most recent development in our evolutionary history. It is the part responsible for processing complex stimuli, thinking through problems, and for language. The neocortex is just a few millimetres thick, and in terms of the relative space that these structures take up, our brains are more primitive than we would like to think. We are driven more by the ancient central areas of the brain and our deep-seated primary consciousness than the conscious processes of which we are actually aware.

One of our primary emotions is fear, and this is an effective survival mechanism originating in the limbic system of the mammalian brain that evolved over 200 million years ago. The emotion we call 'fear' produces the flight/fight response in our nervous system when the release of adrenaline causes the heart to beat faster and increases blood flow to the muscles. This happens automatically in the subconscious, since this is a much faster response than waiting for conscious awareness, which could be too slow to enable you to escape from a predator. This is why you sometimes jump when you sense something is there, but before you know what it actually is. It can also be a cause of phobias in people.

Throughout our evolutionary history, we have responded subconsciously to threats in the environment such as poisonous spiders and snakes or predatory animals such as lions. We are also predisposed to fear stimuli connected with disease, such as substances that are perceived as dirty, and animals associated with decay (e.g. maggots and worms). A fear of reptiles such as snakes or crocodiles is an ancient one. When the mammalian brain was first evolving, reptiles were the biggest threat, so an ancient fear of them is deeply embedded in our limbic system. In modern society we have dangers such as electricity and roads, and yet we do not see phobias associated with these things (although of course you may be afraid of electricity following an accident with it). True phobias occur when we experience irrational fears because conscious reasoning is overruled by subconscious conditioning over millions of years of evolution.

As human beings, we have evolved a large brain and, with it, *secondary consciousness*, which gives us the capacity for self-awareness and abstract thinking. This allows us to examine our motivations and influence their outcome. Humans are social animals, and to be left alone is dangerous in evolutionary and survival terms. An individual alone is vulnerable to predators, and it is easier to hunt or collect food in groups rather than alone – both compelling reasons to stay as part of a group. Self-awareness is vital therefore for evaluating the feelings and predicting the responses of others in the social group so that we are not expelled from it. To be aware of and understand the intricacies of our interactions with others also allows us to relate much more successfully with them, and consciousness is likely to have preceded language and an ability to speak to one another.

Secondary consciousness begins to develop in humans from the age of about two, when children recognize themselves in a mirror. Research suggests that this secondary consciousness may also be present to a degree in chimpanzees and dolphins, since they show 'mirror self-recognition'. Dolphins were shown to exhibit self-awareness during a series of experiments when captive dolphins were marked with a felt pen on areas of the body they could only see with the aid of a mirror. Their pool had a variety of surfaces along the walls, but the marked dolphins went to the mirror to look at the mark. If the dolphins were 'marked' with a sham pen (which did not actually leave a mark) they lost interest in their reflection much quicker than if they had a real mark on their bodies. Both dolphins and chimps are social animals who benefit in survival terms by staying together. So it seems that secondary consciousness may have evolved as a survival mechanism in social animals. We do not have complex capabilities such as language because we have bigger brains or more neurons than other animals but because evolution has shaped our brain through natural selection to become more efficient, increasing our chances of survival and reproductive success. Our secondary consciousness evolved because we are a social species.

Does all this mean that our behaviour and our lives are simple mechanistic responses to threats in the environment and that we do not have free will? Are we just biological robots with no purpose other than to reproduce and survive? We are undoubtedly a product of evolution, but there is plenty of scope for free will. Philosophy professor Daniel Dennett recently put forward a compelling argument for the existence of free will in humans as an evolutionary adaptation. His hypothesis is far from the restrictive view traditionally held by science that we are simply a collection of biological parts, which work like a machine within the confines of scientific and natural laws. It seems that free will does exist, and we have a great many choices about the way we live our lives, not only within modern society, but throughout our evolutionary history.

As secondary consciousness evolves and we become more sophisticated in our ability to interact with others and make conscious decisions, I suspect our degree of free will increases. We are in the most fortunate times of all in our long evolutionary history – to be able to make conscious decisions about our lives and to use our free will to change the circumstances we find ourselves in. Science is clearly moving forward and expanding its views about the nature of consciousness, and even though we may never completely understand it, we can use this knowledge of the brain and our consciousness in order to improve our lives considerably.

The subconscious mind

Your conscious mind is the objective, reasoning, logical part of your brain where decisions are made. It interacts with the outside world and learns from the experience it receives via your five senses. In contrast, your subconscious does not reason things out or monitor your thoughts, good or bad; it simply accepts conscious decisions and thought patterns and acts upon them. Your subconscious mind accepts suggestions whether they are true or false. This is why hypnotists are able to make their subjects behave in bizarre ways. The subjects' subconscious temporarily accepts the suggestions and acts upon them.

It is also why subliminal suggestions in advertising are so effective – they appeal directly to the subconscious mind. In fact, they are so effective that subliminal messages have been banned from advertising since the 1950s. A psychoanalyst called Lloyd Silverman developed subliminal therapy, known as subliminal psychodynamic activation (SPA), during the 1960s and 1970s. This early work has been developed in various ways since then, and the subconscious or unconscious mind is an important part of traditional psychoanalytic theory and modern psychotherapy.

During the 1980s, the concept of the cognitive unconscious described the process of progressive automation whereby conscious thoughts are transferred to the subconscious mind. This has been seen during scanning and shows a burst of activity affecting several areas of the brain, which reduce with repetition. This actually shows the brain transferring conscious activity and thoughts into subconscious memory. The brain reduces repeated tasks to subconscious habits in order to free up more space in the brain for conscious processing, a vital survival mechanism (without which we would experience sensory overload).

You can experience this progressive automation yourself when you learn a new task such as driving a car. At first you need to consciously think about depressing the accelerator, moving your foot on to the brake, steering and looking in the mirror, but with practice you begin to do all these tasks automatically and they become second nature. Your conscious brain then becomes free to make decisions and process other information while your subconscious effectively allows you to drive the car. This unconscious processing goes on when you repeatedly undertake a task or think a thought. This is the basis of habits, and your subconscious does not discriminate between good or bad habits; it is just a mechanism to keep your conscious awareness free for more immediate tasks.

Conscious thought, as we have seen, is automated into your subconscious since you cannot consciously remember everything at once. Your conscious brain needs to remain free to concentrate on immediate matters, particularly its interaction with the environment and making decisions. However, thoughts processed and stored in your subconscious are not lost, and turning your conscious attention back to those thoughts can reverse the process. In other words, your memory is recalled.

Sometimes it takes time for your brain to recall information, and psychologists call this lag the 'incubation period'. Often when we struggle to remember something such as someone's name, we give up on it, and then it mysteriously pops into our mind. If we are grappling with a problem we cannot solve with our conscious mind, we are advised to 'sleep on it' and often the solutions come to us when we stop thinking so hard about it – sometimes as a dream, sometimes as a feeling of simply 'knowing'. This is our subconscious processes (or our intuition) working beneath our conscious awareness and it is an important mechanism.

Scientists and artists have used unconscious processes to find solutions to problems and inspire creativity throughout the ages. Fredrich Kekule, a chemist, solved the structure of the benzene ring when he had a dream of hydrogen and carbon atoms joining together in a circle. Einstein dreamed he was riding on a beam of light when he came up with his theory of relativity, and artists and composers have famously used their subconscious intuition to inspire creativity. Mozart's compositions popped into his mind in their finished form, often while his conscious attention was on something completely different, and the Russian composer Dmitri Shostakovich could hear music when he tilted his head to one side. This was the result of an injury during the First World War when a splinter of metal became lodged in his brain. It probably activated his auditory brain structures when he tilted his head and he used much of the music he heard in his mind in his compositions.

The benefits of tapping into the subconscious mind can be seen in learning and memory. Evidence for learning during sleep has been accumulating for the past 25 years, but much of the evidence for this had come from the use of anaesthetics. While under anaesthesia, patients have reported hearing the conversations of the theatre staff during operations, and recalled such conversations accurately when they came round from the anaesthetic. Similar occurrences have been reported in out-of-body and near-death experiences. These experiences suggest that the unconscious brain is aware of its surroundings and is able to remember.

In the 1960s, in one experiment researchers tested the subconscious learning ability of patients under anaesthesia by playing information tapes to them when they were anaesthetized. Compared to their conscious recall of knowledge prior to surgery (37 per cent), their recall rose dramatically after surgery (62 per cent). Studies since this one have also found evidence of learning during anaesthesia. The subconscious, it seems, is always vigilant and aware, even when our conscious awareness is temporarily switched off.

When you consciously convey an idea to your subconscious mind, an impression or pattern is made on your brain cells. Your subconscious cannot distinguish between what is real or vividly imagined, and once it accepts an idea it will begin to execute it in reality. This acceptance of an idea is important. Your subconscious will use the laws of nature, associate ideas and use all your past knowledge to attract the circumstances you desire, but to make lasting changes, we have to believe in ourselves, and our capabilities. If you don't really believe in something, it will be in conflict with your subconscious acceptance of it, and you will ultimately scupper your own efforts to change. To be effective, suggestions to your subconscious mind have to be aligned with your principles and beliefs.

3

Mind–body connections

Biofeedback

Biofeedback is a technique in which people are trained to use the physiological signals from their body to improve health. Your brain and body continually converse via electrochemical messages with a highly sensitive biofeedback mechanism. Just the simple act of keeping your balance involves reflexes that require feedback from your eyes, inner ear and sensory nerves in muscles and joints, and hormones continuously monitor and adjust body functions such as metabolism, water balance, blood sugar levels and sex hormones.

Professor Emeritus Neal Miller is the 'father' of biofeedback and maintains that the body and brain are not simply connected, but exist and act as a unit. We are aware we have voluntary control over our motor functions such as movements of limbs and muscles, but until recently medical science believed that nearly all other bodily functions, such as blood flow, body temperature and endocrine control, were under *involuntary* regulation and beyond our conscious control. However, Dr Miller and others have found, through studies of biofeedback, that this is not the case. Conditions such as diabetes, Raynaud's disease, raised intraocular pressure, cerebral palsy and even cancer have been helped with biofeedback. It is also used to train people to control their own brain waves. Michael Tansey, a psychologist, trained children with learning disabilities to exercise the brain circuitry of the parts of the cortex involved in learning by voluntarily increasing brain wave activity, which was monitored using an EEG. These results, among others, showed an improvement in hand–eye co-ordination, improved fine motor control, greater memory capability and increased IQ scores. These experiments were repeated and the results verified by other researchers in over 150 similar learning-disabled children.

Biofeedback has been studied extensively by scientists, and over 10,000 scientific papers demonstrating its effectiveness have been published. Biofeedback can be used as a therapy, and has been successful in treating over 150 medical and psychological disorders. Physiological activity in the body can be measured scientifically using electromyography (EMG), which measures muscle activity, changes in blood flow through changes in skin temperature, changes in the skin such as sweating (which tracks emotions) and changes in electroencephalogram (EEG) readings which monitor brain activity. Heart rate, respiration and gastrointestinal activity can also be monitored very simply to measure biofeedback. A polygraph or lie detector also measures biofeedback by detecting changes in the galvanic response of the skin – its ability to conduct electricity – which gives a measure of whether a person is tense (associated with lying) or relaxed (associated with telling the truth). The same response is seen when threat or arousal are present and the polygraph will jump when a person remembers a past trauma.

An astonishing experiment by Cleve Backster, a polygraph expert, showed that living cells removed from the body, attached to a polygraph and placed in another room, still react to a stimulus when the person does. If the results of this experiment are right, it is further evidence that our mind and body act as a unit.

People who use biofeedback techniques can improve their health and well-being, lower their blood pressure and heart rate, strengthen their immune response, and it has even been known for people to improve (or even cure) their cancer and other diseases through biofeedback. Your brain triggers this physiological cascade of reactions to make what you vividly imagine a reality, since it uses the same neural networks. You can use these techniques to change your feelings and beliefs. Use your imagination to create visualizations – they are a powerful biofeedback mechanism. When you realize that you are in complete control of your thinking process, the possibilities for dramatic improvements in your life are limitless.

How we link with the universe

To understand our true nature, we have to have an appreciation of our place in the universe.

We are part of the universe and are subject to its universal laws, which hold it all together and keep it running smoothly. This means physical laws that are grounded in scientific theory, such as gravity and electromagnetism, as well as natural laws, which seek balance such as cause and effect.

We are born from the stars in a very literal sense since our bodies are made up of elements that are produced in stars: carbon, hydrogen, nitrogen, oxygen and traces of other elements. Our own solar system and our home, planet Earth, formed from elements that were made in stars and ejected in supernova explosions in space. We are an interconnecting and ever-changing part of the world around us, and even as we breathe we are exchanging elements such as carbon with trees and plants. When you eat, you ingest elements from the soil, plants and animals, and these become incorporated into the cells and atoms of your body. Each of us is exchanging particles on a physical level with our breath, so that everything in the universe is interconnected.

Your whole body continuously replaces the elements it is made up of throughout your life, so that by old age, it is almost totally different in composition from the body you were born with. When you die, the elements you are made of break down and go back into the earth to be recycled. Elements are recycled throughout the universe, and it is probable that even now you have, within you, particles of creatures that lived on Earth millions of years ago. You could have atoms of dinosaurs, or the first humans, in your own body.

Since the Earth was formed, some 4.6 billion years ago, the same water has been recycled over and over again by evaporation and condensation, and even the continents are recycled through erosion, subduction and volcanism. The oxygen we breathe is recycled through plant photosynthesis. The universe and the world around us are always changing, always interacting. When the Native Americans say that the trees are our brothers and sisters, they are correct in a very real sense. We really are a microcosm of the wider universe. Our bodies and our very consciousness are an integral and interacting part of the universe around us.

When we hurt each other or planet Earth, we hurt ourselves too. If societies around the world would realize this at a fundamental level, perhaps we could start to rebalance the destruction caused by modern human beings. Humankind has wreaked havoc with the environment, systematically caused the extinction of other species and, as a future consequence, may well extinguish our own human existence in the process. The astonishing stupidity of mankind leaves me breathless sometimes! I guess that's a subject for another book, but it illustrates the fact that we have ultimate control over our reality, even on a global scale.

How we create our own reality

All around us, and within our own bodies, there is change. Nothing stays the same and everything is interlinked and interdependent. And nothing is apparently as it seems! We perceive our physical reality in a particular way through our senses, and our brain creates its own reality through the signals it receives through our eyes, ears, nerve endings and taste buds. We don't have the same perception of the world as other living things. Even time and space are perceived differently in other species. We don't see the magnetic contours in the Earth's crust, yet other creatures see it and use it to navigate. We don't see photon particles or waves without special equipment; we just see light within our own visible spectrum. Our brain's reality is different, even to another human being with the same senses. We all perceive the world in a slightly different way and we also interpret our perceptions differently. One person is afraid of spiders, another keeps them as pets; one person sees beautiful flowers, another sees weeds. The world is a very different place depending on where you are 'coming from', your perceptions, or the way your brain is wired via your neural networks. That, as we have seen, is dependent on your learning and your thoughts.

We see and feel solid shapes and things around us, yet matter is made up of atoms, which largely consist of empty space. An atom consists of a dense nucleus surrounded by a cloud of electrons. To give you an idea of the size of an atom compared to the nucleus, imagine the M25 ring road around London, which is around 40 kilometres in diameter, as the size of the atom. The nucleus would be the size of a London taxi, around 4 metres across! It is mainly empty space. The desk at which I am working at the moment is made up mainly of the empty space within its atoms, and our own bodies too are far from being composed of solid matter.

All this means is that in a very real sense our *thoughts are our reality*. We become what we predominantly think about. We attract the things we want to us by our intentions and thoughts. This is not just some sort of weird 'psychobabble', it is real at the level of the quantum field, and in the plasticity of the way our brains learn and develop. We can physically attract the things we want in our lives by our intentions and desires. If you continually think about being broke, you'll stay broke. If you think you're hopeless at maths, then you will be. If you believe with conviction that you can be successful, then you can – with the right application of intention, desire and correct action.

Quantum theory meets neuroscience

When you consider matter at a subatomic level, it gets even more bizarre. Atoms are not fundamental particles, but are made up of quantum particles (there may be even more fundamental particles yet to be discovered). Quantum particles are infinitesimally small 'bits' of information and energy, which behave in extraordinary ways. Quantum particles can appear and disappear in an instant, appear in two places at the same time, and communicate instantaneously over vast distances. Their behaviour is strange to say the least, and they don't seem to fit our current theories of physics, particularly gravity, at all. Scientists are making huge efforts to find a 'theory of everything' to account for these strange quantum effects in our understanding of the universe.

Our bodies, according to our current understanding of matter, are ultimately made up of quantum particles or 'bits' of energy and information:

Einstein's famous equation, $E=MC^2$, states that Energy is = to Mass x Constant squared
(the constant is the speed of light in a vacuum: 3×10^8 ms^{-1},
or 186,291 miles per second)

What this means is that energy is interchangeable with matter, so the solid things around you, including your body, exist as matter and energy interchangeably without contravening the laws of physics and the conservation of energy. They are not really solid at all; they consist of quantum energy and information, which vibrates at a particular frequency. Our relatively limited senses perceive the vibrations as solid objects, much as your brain 'fills in the gaps' when watching a television screen, which really consists of a collection of dots. So everything in the universe, including you and me, is at its fundamental level a pattern of vibrating quantum energy and information. Solid matter is just an illusion of our senses and a result of the way that our brain interprets the signals it receives.

Our consciousness too consists of a collection of energy and information particles arising from the quantum field. The quantum field of energy and information is simply pure potential. It is manifested as the matter we recognize simply by our observation of it. Potential energy and information 'collapses' in the direction of our intention when we observe it. In other words, we as observers can influence the nature of matter purely by our thoughts and intentions. We have conscious control over our own reality. Matter and energy are 'versatile' and can be moulded by our consciousness. This takes time and the application of sustained attention because the relatively dense field of matter reacts more slowly than our thoughts. This sounds very philosophical, and completely counterintuitive, like the question of whether the grass is still green when you are not looking at it, but it is backed up by scientific theory and experimental evidence in the field of quantum mechanics.

All this has fascinating and profound implications for the way we interact with the world around us and the way we view our beliefs and capabilities. It takes a paradigm shift to appreciate it, but it has life-changing effects when you do.

So how does quantum theory meet neuroscience? Your brain is an amazingly intricate piece of biological equipment and, theoretically at least, it may be able to harness the infinite energy and information of the quantum field (some refer to this as the infinite intelligence or universal consciousness). Quantum particles may interact with the biological matter of your brain, giving rise to conscious experience. Every minute of every day zillions of quantum particles called neutrinos pass, totally unnoticed, through your body without interacting with it at all. In fact, they pass through the Earth and on into space as if there were nothing there. Quantum particles permeate space and time and are around and within us constantly. So it is plausible that some kind of quantum particle actually interacts with the biological tissue of our brains and nervous systems and may give rise to consciousness.

In fact, an influential theory of the neural correlates of consciousness was developed by Roger Penrose, a quantum physicist, and Stuart Hameroff, an anaesthesiologist. They formulated a hypothesis that quantum particles interact within the microtubules of the cytoskeleton, present in every cell of the body, including the brain cell or neuron, as a basis for consciousness. The cytoskeleton consists of tiny hollow structures, and these function as a support and transport system for the cell. The microtubules within the neurons in the brain are connected with every part of the neural network and are involved in all neural functions and information processing throughout the brain, giving rise to a unified state of conscious experience. Hameroff's work on anaesthetics has contributed insights into how consciousness is temporarily 'knocked off' by anaesthetic agents. He proposed that anaesthetics cause structural changes in brain proteins, which interfere with the mobility of electrons, thereby disrupting consciousness.

4

Your brain and behaviour

It is, to me, a sign of our deepening consciousness as human beings that we are able to investigate in ever-increasing detail the fascinating behaviour of our own and other species, to ponder the reasons for our existence, and of the intricacies of our biology.

Many neuroscientists today study the mechanisms in the brain that result in the expression of behaviour in an individual. Properly called *behavioural neuroscience*, this discipline examines the neurobiological processes that underlie behaviour and essentially looks at the 'hardware' of the brain and how this relates to behaviour – in other words, how the central nervous system translates a stimulus into behavioural activity.

Traditionally, the behavioural sciences have used a 'software' explanation of behaviour. They study the stimulus from the environment that generates behaviour without considering the mechanisms in the brain that generate that behaviour – for example, the salivating reflex of Pavlov's dogs, when a bell is rung in association with food, is a 'software' explanation. Behavioural neurobiology would also take into account the neuronal activity in the brain to explain the dog's response to food and the ringing bell. It's a bit like studying the inner workings of a computer and its hard drive in order to understand how it produces letters, words and pictures on the screen rather than just knowing what it does when you press a certain key. Essentially, the 'software' explanation is the approach used traditionally by behavioural psychology and other behavioural science disciplines, which look at the psychological responses of individuals to events in their lives.

While this approach is tried and tested and can be invaluable for the treatment of many psychological problems, behavioural neurobiology takes a more holistic approach to behavioural responses in the individual by including the mechanisms of the brain and its neuronal activity. While the discipline does not have the answers to our complex human psychological problems, in this book I am applying the principles of behavioural neurobiology to further our discussion of the way our brains think and how we can use that knowledge to improve our lives. Behavioural neuroscience is at the cutting edge of investigation into the behaviour of animals and uses the latest developments in neuroscience and ethology (the study of natural behaviour).

Significant advances in behavioural neurobiology were made in the 1970s and 1980s, as a result of emerging neurobiological scientific methods of investigation and a new focus on behaviour by scientists in the field of both behavioural research and neuroscience. In 1975, a prominent biologist, Edward O. Wilson, predicted the success of behavioural neurobiology as a scientific discipline. Now and in the future it is set to flourish and influence the scientific community. Human behaviour is also generated at the neuronal level in the brain. We can only do what our brains allow us to do. The incredible thing is that we have control over our thinking processes because of our self-awareness, or secondary consciousness, and this has profound implications in our quest to improve our lives.

We are the sum total of our lives to date. Our brains and minds hold the patterns formed in our neurons, which we have been developing since childhood. Our neural networks hold our unique memories and associations. Some are very firmly established with deep pathways, while others have a more tenuous hold; but all these patterns and networks are the result of repetitions and habits of thought, and it is these that form the basis of our behaviour and responses.

Overcoming past conditioning

We all live with the results of our past conditioning, from childhood on into our adult lives. Some of this conditioning is deeply entrenched and causes us problems, while other parts can be overcome more easily by consciously changing our habits of thought and our thinking processes. There are many good books available as a starting point to enable you to tackle specific problems, but if you feel you have a serious problem that you cannot tackle alone, I recommend a course of counselling. Most counsellors and therapists use a general 'eclectic' approach, meaning that they draw on many different forms of therapy to suit their clients. There are also many specialist counsellors (such as for eating disorders, relationship problems, family specialists, etc.) who may be able to help you explore and make sense of your problems.

It is extremely liberating to finally understand a particular problem that has adversely affected your life, sometimes for many years. This understanding is often enough to motivate you to make necessary changes in your life, although further help in the form of psychotherapy or behavioural therapy can be sought if necessary. Sometimes we fail to take control of our lives and make the changes we want to make because we become 'stuck' with past conditioning and old beliefs, which are no longer appropriate in our current circumstances. Because of this, I have included the next section on the different approaches that have been used over the years in making behavioural changes through psychotherapy, and hope to convince you that you can overcome problems and past conditioning quickly and effectively using the latest methods of neuropsychology.

Types of psychotherapy

There are over 400 individual types of therapy offering different approaches to psychotherapy, and although it is beyond the scope of this book to explore them all fully, an appreciation of psychotherapy and the traditional ways people use the 'software' of the psychological approach to overcome problems and change behaviour will give perspective to the ideas in this book about the role of neuroscience, and the truly phenomenal personal power you have available to you right now to change your life using nothing but your own brain and mind. The following is a brief summary of the traditionally accepted forms of psychotherapy offered within the psychological sciences, along with some illustrative case histories.

Psychoanalysis

Psychoanalysis is a form of therapy that aims to uncover unconscious motivations and impulses using the free association of ideas and the interpretation of dreams. It was developed by Sigmund Freud. He suggested, in his theory of personality, that anxiety is caused by unconscious conflicts that can usually be traced back to childhood. He believed that unacceptable, often sexual, urges from early childhood, as well as repressed feelings and impulses, lead to anxiety, a theory that has caused some controversy.

Humanistic and Gestalt therapy

Humanistic therapy was developed by Carl Rogers in the 1940s and it became a major alternative to psychoanalysis. Humanistic therapy starts from the basic assumption that people are good and have innate worth, and that psychological problems represent some type of block to one's potential for personal growth. Therapy aims to release this block.

Gestalt therapy, like the client-centred therapy developed by Rogers, was founded because of disenchantment with traditional psychoanalysis. Fritz Perls was trained in the techniques of Freud, but broke away to develop his own ideas. In 1969 he founded Gestalt therapy, which places the emphasis exclusively on the present experiences of the client rather than the past, and encourages clients to 'get in touch' with bodily sensations and emotions that they may have been unaware of for some time. Gestalt therapy can often be very confrontational and challenging to the client as they are urged to deal honestly with their emotions.

Behavioural therapies

Joseph Wolpe is one of the founders of behavioural therapy, and held the basic assumption that people learn maladaptive behaviour in the same way as they learn adaptive behaviour. In other words, undesirable behaviour is the actual problem, not a reflection of the problem, and can be unlearned. There are several specific approaches to behavioural therapy, such as systematic desensitization and cognitive behavioural therapy:

Systematic desensitization

Developed by Wolpe, this has proved successful in treating phobias. After learning relaxation techniques, the client is then exposed to increasing levels of the stimulus that elicits fear.

In contrast, a technique called *flooding* attempts to rid the client of fear by flooding the senses with the fear stimulus until their response is desensitized. In other words, after encountering the most frightening scenario of all, the client learns that there is nothing to fear and the phobia subsides.

Elsa

Elsa had a phobia about spiders and was willing to undergo behavioural therapy since she wanted to go on holiday to the Caribbean, but was afraid there would be a lot of very large spiders out there. She didn't want to spoil the holiday for her husband, Ted, so she was prepared to try the technique of flooding. Elsa's therapist, Sue, explained the procedure, and although Elsa felt a rush of fear at the thought of being exposed to the spiders, she agreed to try it. So Elsa, Ted and Sue went along to the local zoo, where they had arranged a visit behind the scenes at the spider enclosures. Sue described the spiders they were about to meet in graphic detail as they slowly made their way inside a darkened room lined with glass cages.

They were greeted by a knowledgeable zookeeper, Joe. Elsa felt extremely anxious as she entered the room. Her legs were shaking and her mouth was dry with fear, but gradually as they strolled around the room, viewing the spiders through the glass, Elsa began to realize that her fear was irrational and that there was no danger in simply looking at the spiders. After just ten minutes, her fear began to subside and she even became quite interested in one or two spiders, asking questions about them.

Next, Sue suggested she take a very brave step and actually touch a spider. Once again, Elsa felt afraid. It was one thing to look at them, but the thought of actually *touching* one was terrifying. She glanced at Ted, who gave her an encouraging smile, and she reluctantly agreed. The zookeeper opened a glass tank and lifted out a large black tarantula. He explained that there was no danger as the spider's fangs had been removed, and then demonstrated this by stroking the spider that sat quietly on his hand.

With much encouragement from everyone, Elsa tentatively reached out and touched the tarantula, her heart beating wildly. The spider sat quietly on the zookeeper's hand, not moving. Elsa recoiled at first, only touching the spider momentarily, but gradually – over a few minutes – she touched it for longer periods until she too was able to stroke it.

In just 15 minutes, Elsa had begun to conquer her fear of spiders by realizing that even the worst imaginable encounter is tolerable. She had also learned not to fear her own anxiety attacks.

Cognitive behavioural therapy (CBT)

This focuses on changing the client's thoughts, beliefs and perceptions. Unlike psychotherapy, cognitive behavioural therapists do not focus on childhood events and experiences, but on the present life of the client. CBT aims to change cognitive (thinking) processes by a variety of methods – including challenging a client's beliefs.

Tom

Tom underwent cognitive behavioural therapy in order to try to overcome his deep and long-lasting depression. He had lost his job as a factory supervisor six months previously and had sunk into a depressed state, unable to motivate himself to look for another job. His wife despaired of him, and eventually gave up trying to help. Finally, she left him for another man. Tom became even more deeply depressed, believing that these events had ruined his whole life and that he had no control over them.

During therapy, Tom came to see that it was not the events that had caused his depression, but his *reaction* to them – the beliefs he held about the events. He realized that he could retrain for a better job as a plumber, and became very enthusiastic about this new job. He also discovered that his wife was taking a renewed interest in him now that his depression was lifting and he was taking action to change his life. Tom still had a long way to go, but he had hope for the future and now believed he had control over his life.

One approach to CBT is to encourage someone with emotional traumas to write about them. Recent research shows that writing provides an outlet for negative thoughts and feelings that a person is inhibited about expressing verbally, and that it improves coping mechanisms, physical and emotional health, as well as immune system functioning in extremely distressed individuals.

Behavioural problems often originate and persist because of past experience or events, but behavioural therapy can often eliminate these problems without delving into the past. For example, a child may begin to wet the bed with all the accompanying guilt and frustration experienced by the child and his family. But instead of delving into family relationships and past experiences as traditional psychotherapy would advocate, a behavioural therapist would install a bell that rings if the child starts to wet the bed. The child wakes and goes to the toilet, and thereby a new habit forms where he does not wet the bed. His relationships with his family improve, and positive reinforcement encourages this new behaviour.

Group therapy

This was common during the Second World War when the stress of war resulted in many psychological problems and psychotherapists were unable to cope with the demand. Group therapy was developed to enable more people to be treated at once, but became an effective form of therapy in itself and social pressure between members of the group often reinforced behavioural changes. Sharing problems is known to help people to cope, and seeing others with similar problems helps a person to gain insight into his own problems. Group therapy has proved useful for alcoholism and other addictions, as well as in helping people cope with grief and bereavement.

Family and couples therapy

This aims to improve relationships in families or couples by observing interactions and then substituting maladaptive interactions with more effective ones. The therapist may suggest that all members of the family must change if there is to be a real improvement, and therapy involves supporting and educating the family as they work through the changes that are necessary.

Parental conditioning

This can be one factor that prevents people from achieving what they want to achieve in life. During childhood, we can be influenced by our parents and environment in a number of ways. These influences can be passed down through the generations and, typically, a parent's approach has been learnt from *their* parents. One study has shown that there are five key 'drivers' that are learnt through parental conditioning, which can be simplified in terms of the following 'statements' that may drive behaviour in adulthood:

1 'Be brave'
2 'Be perfect'
3 'Please me'
4 'Hurry up'
5 'Don't be better than me'

Eric

Eric experienced significant stress whenever he spent time making door-to-door sales in the course of his job. This was primarily because he felt shy with strangers and felt under pressure to win the respect of these potential customers. What made this worse was the fact that Eric would force himself to do an unreasonable number of hours of sales. This gave him a temporary sense of pride and achievement, but as a consequence his stress was beginning to spiral out of control. Eventually, Eric made himself quite ill from the excessive pressure to which he subjected himself. After a period of therapy, he began to recognize that he had been driving himself to work in this way because of his fundamental belief that the best way to overcome his fears was to 'be brave' and hope for the best. This 'internal driver' is of course not a universal answer to all 'fearful' situations, and Eric had to learn to measure his tolerance to stress and to reprioritize his 'internal drivers'. Eric made the decision that 'looking after himself' was the number one priority. In attempting to 'be brave', he had denied himself the opportunity to ask for help in a number of ways, including asking for emotional support from friends. Eric was also being dishonest with himself about his limitations and trying to 'run before he could walk'. In the future, Eric decided he would get professional advice on how to overcome his shyness and to recognize the factors that made him feel stressed, and address these things one at a time before they spiralled out of control.

Jane

Jane was dissatisfied with her performance at work; it seemed that everything she did was wrong. The pinnacle of her unhappiness was associated with 'public speaking'. Whenever she was presenting information to an audience, she was constantly monitoring herself, looking for mistakes, and was very intolerant of her nerves. Jane became increasingly frustrated with herself and could not live with her poor self-image. After seeking help from a colleague, Jane learnt to recognize that she was trying to 'be perfect' and that she struggled to accept her mistakes. An important step forward was the recognition that an audience actually *like* to see imperfection and mistakes because then they feel as if the presenter is 'more human' and can 'relate to her'.

Jane began to experiment and allowed herself to make mistakes, and even deliberately introduced some mistakes for light entertainment. Jane noticed that her work colleagues became more at ease with her and her presentations became more interactive. As Jane challenged the 'be perfect driver' in other aspects of her job, she began to recognize that all tasks should carry an appropriate level of accuracy and began to adopt the 80/20 rule. An 80 per cent level of completion is probably good enough and will only take 20 per cent of the time; to complete the remaining 20 per cent of a task will often take 80 per cent of the time. In other words, Jane was far more valuable to her firm when she tackled a wider variety of tasks. Even if they were not all perfect, they were 'fit for purpose'.

Does psychotherapy work?

Many thousands of people derive benefit from psychotherapy every year, and without it there would undoubtedly be more confused and unhappy people in the world. Sometimes the chance to talk to someone about a problem clarifies it and allows you to decide your own course of 'psychotherapy'. There is evidence to show that a caring friend can be as effective as professional psychotherapy, and sometimes you need nothing more than to stop and take a hard look at your life in order to make decisions, which allow you to move forward. Occasionally our problems are harder to understand or we can't face them alone, and we turn to psychotherapy for the answers. But does psychotherapy work? The question is important because our approach to our psychological health profoundly affects our outlook on life and our achievements, whether or not we need psychotherapy.

In 1980, a well-known analysis of 475 studies comparing the outcome of older therapies such as Gestalt therapy with the more modern behavioural therapies showed that there is in fact some scientific evidence that most people who voluntarily enter behavioural therapy tend to improve, and that behavioural and cognitive behavioural therapy was much more effective than the older traditional therapies. This was also confirmed in a more recent study in 1990. Behavioural therapists believe that behavioural changes affect cognition – that is, thinking processes – and that introspection and analysis of the past is not enough to bring about changes as the older traditional types of therapy advocate. In other words, analysing past experiences and dwelling on the reasons for maladaptive behaviour is not as successful as changing the beliefs and thinking processes resulting from a person's present emotional state in order to improve psychological problems.

So what are we to make of all this, and what are the implications for the ideas put forward in this book about neuroscience and our ability to rewire our brain in order to bring about change? My own view is that any type of psychotherapy will only be effective if the client really wants it to work, and holds a solid belief that it actually *will* work. This appears to be supported by the scientific studies evaluating psychotherapy, and is also seen in the 'placebo effect' in medication when dummy pills, used in controlled experiments, are as effective as the real thing for bringing about physiological and psychological improvement simply as a result of the belief that they will work.

In order to make lasting changes, we need an overwhelming desire to change, and the belief that it is possible. This often happens when we are so desperately unhappy with the way our lives are going that we will do absolutely anything to change our circumstances. Psychotherapy can be an incredibly valuable support system in this case. When our self-esteem and confidence are at an all-time low, a good therapist can help us to believe in ourselves again and build up the inner strength and courage to make positive changes. Sometimes our problems are so distressing and so personal that we are only prepared to tell a professional about them, so psychotherapy is a vital tool when problems become all-consuming or appear insurmountable.

There may be a negative side to psychotherapy, though, and it is important to be aware of this. While understanding our problems so we can deal with them more effectively is usually a positive step, psychotherapy can sometimes inadvertently encourage us to feel like 'victims'. In other words, once we have a label for our problems, such as anxiety or depression, we 'officially' have a problem. This can encourage self-pity and using our 'problems' as an excuse to remain stuck. Oliver is an example of this type of behaviour.

Oliver

Oliver was diagnosed with depression after being made redundant, and he knew it would take effort on his part to overcome his problems. But instead of trying to get better and find a way out of his depression, he rationalized that it was OK to stay in bed all day instead of making the effort to retrain for another job. He believed that people would consider his behaviour understandable because, after all, a doctor had diagnosed depression. He almost had permission to wallow in his unhealthy behaviour.

It is not uncommon for people to blame their therapists when they are not making progress with behavioural problems. This sort of projection of responsibility by blaming others is very common, but is extremely unproductive in terms of making positive changes. If we feel that someone else is responsible for our problems, we will never take steps to change things for ourselves. This is where desire, motivation and belief is needed in bucketfuls if we are to make positive changes to overcome a problem.

Another downside of psychotherapy is that you can spend months or even years exploring a problem and learning everything about it, but end up going around in circles. In other words, it is possible to understand our problems intimately, yet fail to take sufficient action to change things. We may be under the illusion that we are doing something about it because we are undergoing therapy, but sometimes this can actually work to prevent us from making real and lasting changes.

One way to overcome this is to set a time limit. Realize that it is important to explore your problem in order to understand it, then decide to work on a practical plan to make the fundamental changes you need in order to progress. When you dwell on the problem, you also give it undue prominence over other aspects of your life. Try to understand it within a realistic time-frame, then very firmly move away from the problem and towards the way you want your life to be in the future.

Looking at all this from the perspective of neuroscience, you may remember from earlier in the book that your brain's neural networks are strengthened with use and repetition. As we saw, this is called long-term potentiation (LTP). When you dwell on a problem intensely or over an extended time, such as when you undergo psychoanalysis, you are reinforcing and strengthening the neural networks associated with the problem by the process of LTP. You are giving those associations prominence and literally hard-wiring them into your brain. If you want to make progress with changes in your life, you need to create and strengthen new neural networks associated with your goals, aspirations and dreams, and weaken or eliminate existing ones that are associated with problem areas.

A new approach

Following the early development of modern psychology, psychology as a science moved through Freudian ideas about psychoanalysis to behaviourism, which studies observable behaviour. Gestalt therapy and humanistic therapy emphasized a more positive view of human potential. But all these approaches were based on observable behaviours with concepts such as consciousness outside the realm of psychology.

Then came the cognitive revolution, as it was called, which saw psychologists rebel against the restrictions of psychology and begin to study consciousness, feelings and mental imagery using an approach called information processing, which used the computer as a model of the brain, abandoning the introspective methods of the past.

Following the cognitive revolution, another revolution in psychology, the biological revolution, saw a divergence of interests in all fields, with a renewed interest in the role of biological factors, studying aspects such as the effects of brain damage on behaviour. In the early and mid twentieth century, behaviourism-dominated psychology and the emphasis of biological factors declined because of a lack of knowledge about how the brain controlled behaviour.

With the extraordinary advances in neurobiology during the 1990s, it became possible to study the brain and nervous system to the degree that we can now see the internal structure of the living brain and measure activity in regions as small as a few millimetres while people are thinking, feeling and perceiving. This combination of cognitive psychology and neuroscience, called cognitive neuroscience, holds much promise for understanding behaviour – and perhaps even discovering the neural correlates of consciousness.

And now, on the cutting edge of science, as we mentioned in the Preface, a new discipline is emerging in psychology called *neuropsychology*, which studies psychological function using revolutionary brain mapping techniques. If the traditional software approach of psychology and psychotherapy is inadequate to describe our psychological make-up, we need to understand the thinking processes of the mind and brain from the basic unit of the neuron upwards. We have seen that traditional forms of psychoanalysis show little scientific evidence that they are effective and that simple analysis of past experience is not sufficient to create lasting changes. These approaches have largely been abandoned. Modern cognitive behavioural approaches show more evidence that they are successful, but are still mainly operating with the software of psychology.

Neuropsychology is an exciting new area of study combining the study of the brain and psychology, although it is still mainly concentrating on the effects of brain damage on behaviour. All these disciplines seem to work in separate compartments, which is a common occurrence in scientific study. However, in order to have a powerful integrated system of understanding our psychological make-up so that we can correct faulty thinking, overcome problems and reach our full potential as human beings, we need to combine the hardware approach of neuroscience and brain function with the software approach of cognitive behavioural therapy.

This book aims to do just that. Once you realize you have complete control over the way you think, to the extent that you can actually physically restructure your brain's neural networks, you cease to behave like a victim, engage in blame games, or go round in ever-decreasing circles trying to understand your problems by analysing the past. Instead, you take control of your present emotional state and your attitudes and beliefs and become proactive in your own unique programme of improvement.

Along with an effective psychological approach, your brain's incredible plasticity is the key to overcoming problems and flawed thinking so that you can make profound and permanent changes for the better. The following practical steps can help to put problems into perspective and weaken the LTP that strengthens the neural networks associated with them, so that you can begin the process of creating new neural networks, changing your thinking patterns, and making positive changes in your life. Share these steps with a therapist if you feel that you need support:

1 Understand

We need to have some understanding of the cause of the problem, without dwelling on it. We have already seen that endlessly analysing past experiences and events does not work, and may actually prevent you from making progress. While of course it is important to have some understanding of how the past has influenced your present emotional state and behaviour, you cannot *change* the past. All you have is the way you are in the present, but the significant point is that you have absolute control over your beliefs and thinking processes at every moment. Ask yourself questions about your beliefs, such as: 'Why do I behave the way that I do?', 'What are the consequences of me not changing?' and 'How can I change my beliefs in order to effect changes?' Challenge your beliefs at every stage. To demonstrate this, let's take a very simple example such as smoking:

Dylan (1)

Dylan wanted to give up smoking as it was affecting his health and his relationship with his girlfriend, who was asthmatic and had given him an ultimatum to give up or she would consider leaving him. He wanted to give up and had tried a few times, but was finding it extremely difficult. In order to understand the problem, he looked at his past for clues as to how he developed the smoking habit. Neither of his parents had smoked, but once he had caught his father smoking in secret. His father explained that smoking helped to relieve the stress of his busy job. Dylan got the message from his father that it was OK to smoke in stressful situations, and began smoking during an exam period at school. Several of his friends smoked in secret too, and this added social pressure for Dylan to continue the habit.

Dylan understood the past conditioning that had led him to smoke, but was still unable to stop. He asked himself honestly why he still smoked, and came up with the following: he enjoyed smoking, and he knew he was only really giving up because his girlfriend had asked him to. This led him to question whether he loved her enough to do this. He realized he was lazy about making the effort to give up, and his tendency to procrastinate meant he was always going to start the next day, not today. Dylan was worried about putting on weight if he gave up smoking and, besides, he worked in a stressful job and felt he had to have some

45

relief. However, he believed he could do it if he really wanted to make the effort.

He then starting asking himself about the consequences of not giving up: he decided that he would probably lose his girlfriend as she usually did what she said she would, and her health was at risk because of his smoking. He realized he did love her, and it was not worth losing her just so he could continue to smoke. He knew that if he failed to give up, his health would deteriorate. He already had a smoker's cough in the mornings, and of course knew that smoking was a major cause of lung cancer. He was not prepared to die early just so that he could continue to enjoy his cigarettes. He also knew that he would feel a failure if he did not stop smoking when he knew it was what he really wanted to do.

Dylan then considered how he could challenge his beliefs about his smoking in order to change: he thought he enjoyed smoking, but in reality it often gave him a tight feeling in his chest and a sore throat. He was also conscious of having bad breath and constantly smelling of smoke. Where was the enjoyment in that? He knew he was lazy about giving up, but he also knew that when he made up his mind about something, he worked hard to achieve it. He remembered how hard he had worked to get an important project finished at work. Dylan knew he wasn't really lazy; he was using it as an excuse. He knew that a small effort every day would result in big results if he made the effort to give up. He did tend to procrastinate, but he decided he had thought about giving up smoking for long enough.

Now it was time to do something about it. If he didn't start today, when would he start? Dylan challenged his belief about putting on weight and decided that if he increased his exercise and cut down on junk food, there was no reason why he should pile on the pounds. He thought about the way he used smoking for stress relief and knew that the issue of him smoking was causing more stress than his job ever did. He realized that although this was the reason his father gave for smoking, it didn't mean that Dylan had to follow suit. Besides, his father had a very stressful heart condition now, probably caused through smoking, and Dylan decided he was intelligent enough to make up his own mind about things – he didn't need to follow his father's patterns of behaviour. He decided to find other ways of relieving stress and began to think about taking up a new hobby such as oil painting. With his belief that he could give up smoking if he wanted to, Dylan began to think differently about his behaviour. We could say he experienced a 'paradigm shift', as he began to move away from the ingrained beliefs he had about smoking.

You have to set a time limit on your analysis of the problem since you can't make real progress until you stop dwelling on it. To do this simply reinforces the neural networks associated with the problem, and you give it prominence over other things in your life. You have to weaken these synaptic connections and create and strengthen new networks in order to make permanent changes. So set a realistic time limit on analysing the past and then make a decision to move on.

2 Forgive

Sometimes, feelings of guilt keep us locked in old behaviour patterns and often we don't understand why; we simply experience the guilt. These feelings are linked to our beliefs about past events, and have no basis in reality. In order to move on, we have to forgive others and forgive ourselves.

Dylan (2)

Dylan decided to forgive his father for his unfortunate remarks about smoking all those years ago. He realized that his father also had a set of faulty, ingrained beliefs that kept him hooked on his smoking habit in response to stress. His father was also free to change his beliefs, but had decided to continue smoking. Dylan also forgave himself for taking on the same beliefs as his father. He was young and impressionable when he began smoking, but now he was an adult and could form his own opinions about smoking. He decided he had other things that he valued more than his old beliefs about smoking and stress. He valued his relationship with his girlfriend, his health and self-esteem more than an unhealthy habit.

Dylan decided he couldn't talk to his father about the past because he was now too ill, so he wrote him a long letter. He never sent it, but he felt a great sense of relief at having got the matter off his chest.

Even if we can't make sense of why we need to forgive, just generally forgiving others and ourselves for human error can be very powerful. We are all simply trying to make the best of our lives and behave in the ways we believe are appropriate at the time. Social and parental conditioning often dictates people's behaviour and this itself is subject to change. Society's values change over time, and individuals develop and mature as they go through life, hopefully gaining wisdom with advancing years, so the circumstances of the past may have little relevance to the reality of today. Simply forgiving human frailty and mistakes can help you to move forward. Generally, people are not out to make your life a misery; they are just being human. We all have off days.

Usually we can do this exercise on our own for it to be effective, but occasionally we need to express our forgiveness openly. Talk to the people concerned if it helps, or write letters if you need closure in order to put the past firmly behind you; say sorry if you need to but, most of all, forgive and release yourself from guilt. In other words, do whatever you have to do in order to move on with your life.

3 Distance yourself

In order to change our thinking patterns and rewire our neural networks so that we can change our lives for the better, we need to disengage ourselves from the past. Not only do we need to create some emotional distance from our old ways of thinking and behaving, but we need to weaken the neural networks that keep us entrenched in them. We need to draw a line under the problem and finalize things. A therapist or counsellor might say we need 'closure'.

One way to distance ourselves is to write down our problems and feelings in the form of a journal, diary or autobiography, and recent scientific research suggests that this is very effective. We can get our thoughts out of our heads and on to paper.

Symbolically empty your head of the problems and all the associations you have with them. Imagine you are clearing out your brain of old junk you no longer need. It is cluttering up your thinking, so get rid of it. You might like to have a little ceremony where you burn or bury these notes, a sort of 'funeral' for your problems and a turning point where you decide to move on. Once you lay your problems to rest, they'll have no power to hurt you. If you keep your notes, put them away. It is interesting and usually encouraging to see just how much you have changed when you review old notes about your feelings some years later.

Try to finalize things from the past by announcing changes. Tell people that from now on you will be acting differently. This can be useful for giving up habits such as smoking. Tell everyone you have given up. Not only does this help you to distance yourself from an old pattern of behaviour, but it adds social pressure to help you stick to the change. Nobody wants to be seen to fail.

Are there any physical changes you can make to help you move away from old problems? Is it feasible to move house or get rid of old possessions that remind you of the past? Perhaps you could change your hairstyle, buy some new clothes, and get a new image? The important thing is to get rid of old associations with past problems so that you feel free to change. Simple things like clearing your desk and sorting out old junk can be extremely liberating, and it shows that you mean business.

Dylan (3)
Dylan burned his letter to his father and scattered the ashes in the garden of his parents' home. It was his way of symbolically releasing the past. He also took steps to distance himself from his old smoking habit by throwing out all his ashtrays, his favourite lighter, and of course his remaining cigarettes. He washed all his clothes as they smelled of smoke, and rearranged the furniture in his lounge to reduce the association with smoking in his favourite comfortable armchair. Dylan announced to everyone that he had given up smoking, especially to his girlfriend who was delighted. He distanced himself from his old behaviour and began to think of himself as a non-smoker. Now he was ready to create new neural pathways.

4 Challenge beliefs and create new neural networks
The rest of this book is devoted to how you can take practical steps to create new neural networks and alter thinking patters to help you to find your dreams and aspirations in life. You will be able to put together a practical, workable plan to make it all a reality based on the principles of neuropsychology. First you need to overcome the mind blocks that may be preventing you from changing, then you need to find your dream and discover an exciting alternative route for the future. When you have found your dream, you have to take positive, decisive action to make it a reality, and finally you need to cherish your dream into the future and cope with setbacks. Let's

work together to make your life an incredible journey of discovery, full of exciting possibilities, starting with clearing out those old mind blocks!

5
Mind blocks – what's stopping you?

There are many reasons why people fail – or don't even begin to try to achieve their dreams for a better life. One of the most common reasons why people continue to live unfulfilling lives is that they simply don't know what they want.

People may have vague ideas of things they might like to do, but dismiss them as wishful thinking. Many others simply don't give much thought to what else they could be doing with their lives. They suffer despondency, depression and emptiness without knowing why. Sometimes there is just not a good enough reason to change. Life is all right as it is – not wonderful, but not too bad either. Sometimes you have to hit the bottom pretty hard before you find the motivation to look for something better. Some people may actually know what they want, but put off doing anything about it by procrastinating with a long list of reasons as to why they can't make a start now. These may include:

- belief;
- fear of failure;
- the effort involved;
- other people's opinions;
- not being assertive;
- unrealistic expectations;
- life's lessons and adversity.

Belief

We discussed belief briefly, but it is such an important part of making successful changes to our lives that we need to explore it a little further. There are two kinds of belief: the belief in yourself as a worthwhile human being, and the belief in your ability to achieve success. We are conditioned throughout our lives to believe other people's opinions of us. We hear negative opinions such as 'you're lazy, stupid, fat, you'll never make anything of yourself, you're hopeless'. If we hear these types of comment often enough, our subconscious mind strives to make our behaviour fit the image of ourselves that we've come to believe. If we are lucky, we hear positive things as well, such as 'you're kind, loving, intelligent, handsome, a great parent', and we will believe that too. Usually it is a fair balance of both that we hear, but it is the negative conditioning that adversely affects us. The old skeletons are brought out of the cupboard and get rattled in our faces throughout our lives, and it takes some soul searching to rid ourselves of old conditioned beliefs.

We are a reflection of what we get from the world, but it also works the other way round too. If you believe with real feeling that you are kind, loving and intelligent, then behave accordingly; the world will reflect that back to you. For the world to change and treat you differently, you have to change. If you keep doing what you have always done, you will keep getting what you have always got!

People don't like change and our subconscious mind will always resist it, so we become entrenched in our conditioned beliefs. The good news is, though, that you can change the way you behave without even having to believe it at first. You have to change your beliefs to make lasting changes, but the feedback you get from other people also helps to change your beliefs about yourself. If you act in a confident manner, people will reflect that back and begin to regard you as a confident person. That in turn will increase your confidence and you will begin to believe you are confident. You can 'fake it' until it becomes real if that is what it takes to change the way you interact with the world around you. You get to choose who you are!

People like to pigeonhole you so they can make judgements, which is why everyone wants to know what you 'do' when they first meet you. They want you neatly packaged into their belief system. Try avoiding the question when people ask it – it's not easy! Sometimes I just want to say, 'I "do" lots of things!' We want to be judged by who we are, not necessarily by what we do for a living. When you find the freedom to be your true self, you increase the belief in your worth as a human being and stop worrying about fitting into pigeonholes. You begin to believe you deserve to achieve your dreams. You have as much right to be here as anyone or anything else on the planet and you have the right to build the life you want, regardless of whether it fits in with other people's conventions or belief systems. If you believe you can do it, you can! Build a positive self-image, believe in yourself, and believe in your abilities.

Napoleon Hill, in his book *Keys to Success*, describes how the overwhelming majority of people fail because they confuse belief with wishing. Only 2 per cent of people actually achieve success – 70 per cent merely wish things would change; 10 per cent develop their wishes into desires but still do nothing; 8 per cent develop hope and dare to imagine they might achieve their dreams, yet still take no positive action; 6 per cent translate hope into belief and expect to succeed, but still take no action; 4 per cent crystallize their wishes, desires, hopes and belief into a burning desire and faith that they will achieve their goals – but still fail to act. Only 2 per cent actually make a plan to get what they want and take action to achieve it!

Wishing you *could* change things won't do it. You have to believe things can change, and believe it to the very core of your being. Then you have to specify your goals and take action to achieve them. You have to join the 2 per cent club!

Fear of failure

Fear of failure is a common reason why people are not prepared even to try to make their dreams come true. Failure is a loaded word with such negative connotations, yet failure holds enormous promise and opportunity if we think of it as simply the mechanics of success. When we fail, we are effectively learning how to succeed, as the famous example of Thomas Edison shows. If Edison had given up after the first attempt or even the hundredth, we wouldn't have electric light bulbs now. He persisted until he got it right, using each failure to eliminate every new method he tried, so that each failure took him closer to his goal.

Fear of success is another, more obscure, reason why people procrastinate and fail to make a start at changing their lives. What if we don't want it when we get it – what do we dream of then? Sometimes having an unobtainable dream seems better than having the real thing, and it is important to decide if you really do want your life to be different. Desire and enthusiasm for the thing you want is fundamental to your attaining it. The thing to remember is that success is a journey, not a destination. When you do get there, you often move the goal posts further on to ever higher dreams and ambitions. You will effectively never 'get there'; there will always be bigger challenges to reach for. What is success to you? Do you have a picture of a successful person in your mind?

Many people fear change. They are afraid to alter the status quo, the security of their work, the relationships they have established, yet the one thing we can be sure of in life is that things will change and are changing right now. Nothing is for ever. Isn't it better to be in control of your life and make your own changes than have them forced upon you? People are made redundant or lose their jobs all the time, relationships break down for lots of reasons, and the people we love sometimes die before we do. That's life. It is full of change, whether it is a gradual shift or a cataclysmic transformation. Contemplating life with its ever-changing scenery and facing an unknown future is certainly scary, yet it is also exhilarating and full of exciting possibilities. We are here and we are alive and breathing – let's make the best of it and turn our lives into something truly meaningful. Embrace change and the promise of better things by directing the inevitability of changes in your life towards the things you want, towards your dreams. Don't stay entrenched in those old, negative neural networks in your brain.

Fear is often felt as a rush of emotion, a torrent of hormones coursing through your bloodstream triggered by your nervous system – the fight or flight response that evolved in humans as a survival mechanism in the days when man hunted wild animals (also known as an 'adrenaline rush'). In our modern lives, fear is a common and chronically disabling emotion, frequently sublimated and disguised as insecurity, aggression and anxiety. Fear prevents us from even attempting to achieve our dreams and keeps us trapped in an unfulfilling life of mediocrity.

If you think of the physical feelings that fear produces as just a cocktail of chemicals rushing through your body, you know that the feeling will pass. You can decide to 'feel the fear and do it anyway' (as per Susan Jeffers's wonderful book with these words as the title). You can call upon your logic to rationalize the feeling of fear and decide if you should act on this feeling (e.g. Is the house really burning down? Do you need to escape?) or whether the feeling is simply an ancient biological reaction that is out of context in the situation you are faced with today (i.e. it's not life or death, you're simply asking for a pay rise!). You can choose to ignore the physical feeling of fear (as distinct from intuition) and act on your will and your logic, knowing that once you begin to take action, the physical feeling of fear will dissipate.

I remember my first ever shark dive. I had, just 30 minutes

previously, passed my first diving exam and immediately boarded the boat for the 40-minute journey to the dive site. Throughout the boat ride my anxiety increased until by the time I stood up, kitted out and poised to step into the sea with at least six Caribbean reef sharks circling the boat, I was almost paralysed with the feelings of fear and panic caused by an overload of adrenaline rushing around my body. I was a novice diver, I'd never dived with sharks before, and the warnings and horror stories I'd been told flashed menacingly before me. I had seconds to react – step back into the safety of the boat or 'feel the fear' and jump in anyway. I took a deep breath and jumped. Once I was in the water and the bubbles had cleared, I came face to face with my first shark and I was completely fascinated! The fear drained miraculously away and was replaced with a feeling of awe and excitement. My logic knew that diving with sharks was relatively safe and I had always wanted to do it. By feeling the physical feelings of fear caused by a release of chemicals into my body and deciding to act on my logic instead, I had the most exciting and amazing experience. In fact, I repeated it four times in the couple of days that followed and could barely get enough of the sharks. Since that trip, I've been cage diving with great white sharks and couldn't wait to get in the water with them! If I had made the split-second decision to step back into the boat that day, I would have missed the most wonderful experiences and it would have been most definitely detrimental to my career as a marine biologist. I'm so very glad I jumped!

Of course, things don't always work out so well. Earth is a very dangerous place – lots of people die or are injured here! But if you can get through being born, you've done one of the most dangerous things you can ever do. By the time you die, you'll have done lots of dangerous things throughout your life even if you don't take up shark diving as a hobby. Simply crossing the road is dangerous, and even if you sat at home in the armchair too paralysed with fear to attempt to do anything at all, you will be hardening your arteries and that in itself is very dangerous – it can cause heart attacks! You are here and you are alive. You have to live your life and you have to be doing something, so you may as well spend your time doing something you love. What is the alternative? Do you want to spend around seventy years or more dragging yourself through day after day of wishing things were different until you run out of time and your life is over? Of course not, that's just waiting to die – but it is sadly what so many people actually do. They live unfulfilled and mediocre lives dreaming dreams that will never be realized, because they allow fear to have the upper hand. You are different. You could have the courage to put your dreams above your fears and live the life you really want.

The effort involved

People often say to me, 'You're so lucky', and I guess I am, but I feel like replying, 'Yes, and the harder I work, the luckier I get!' We don't get where we are by pure luck. Good things don't usually come to us on a plate; we have to plan for them and earn them. Sometimes it seems as if we had a lucky break, but this is often preparedness met with opportunity. Luck implies we did nothing to deserve the things we get, and that is often simply not true. The grass always looks greener on the other side, but it probably took a lot of effort to get it that way. We just see the 'finished product' – the results. Richard Branson didn't just wake up one morning with a business empire in place. He built it up day by day and undoubtedly spent a great deal of time and effort at it, making many mistakes along the way. What makes him a great entrepreneur is his courage and determination to find a way to make it work. Very few have such fortitude.

When people consider what would be involved in making their dreams come true, it simply seems like too much effort. Why give up cosy evenings in front of the television for a class to learn a new skill? Why bother to set up that business you've always dreamed of, when the risks seem overwhelming? Well, the old adage is true – you don't get something for nothing in this life and sometimes you have to make an extraordinary effort to get anywhere at all. Even then, things may not work out the way you planned. So what is the alternative? Remain in your comfort zone, and stay unhappy, broke, disgruntled and wishing things would change? Being alive is an effort. We all have to provide for our basic needs of shelter, warmth and food, and if you want your life to mean something as well, it takes a great deal of extra effort to achieve this, doesn't it?

Strangely enough, the answer is 'not necessarily'. When you are working towards something meaningful and worthwhile to you, when you are on track to achieving your dream life, it is not an effort, it becomes a magical journey of discovery when you look forward to every day and happily spend your time pursuing your special goals. You lose yourself in your own world and time stands still. Effort is having to 'go to work' every day to a job you hate with no purpose other than to bring home a survival wage. That's being trapped in the rat race, and who can be happy when they feel trapped and unfulfilled? To be free and living the life you've always dreamed of is effortless.

Other people's opinions

We have already seen that people don't always think through their opinions. If people disapprove of what you are trying to do, it doesn't mean a great deal anyway. Human beings' opinions can and do change over time; people change their opinions like they change their underwear in order to be accepted by others. So many people slink around, scrutinizing their opinion and checking that it will be acceptable before they speak or act. This is simply insecurity and the fear of being disliked.

Don't go around apologizing for yourself. All this does is build resentment and disrespect. Have the courage to run your own life and disregard the opinions of others. You don't have to explain your every move – and don't expect other people to justify themselves to you either. Usually, if people want you to know something, they will tell you about it – you don't need to pry. No one else can live your life for you or learn the unique lessons you will learn. So proudly start to love who you really are and openly be yourself, and you will miraculously feel a lot happier. And, as a bonus, you will gain self-respect and the respect of others. No one can make you feel inferior or unhappy without your permission.

Becoming more assertive

Being assertive means standing up for your rights, wants and needs without violating those of others. It is the ideal position and allows you to say 'no' to unreasonable requests so that you can manage your time effectively. Your position with others is dynamic, and the reactions of others often depend on the situation and on their own communication skills, but being assertive leads to high self-esteem, increased confidence and improved communication (see Figure 5). By increasing your self-esteem and your confidence, you are likely to take more initiatives and improve your chances of success in making the desired changes in your life.

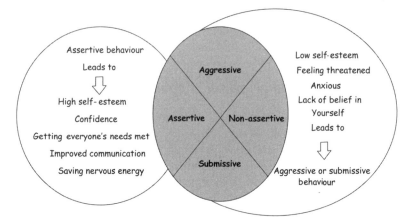

Figure 5 Types of behaviour and self-esteem

Both aggressive and non-assertive or submissive behaviour often originate from low self-esteem. Self-esteem is your own evaluation of yourself; your worth as a person, and your beliefs about yourself as a competent, worthwhile human being. Aggressive behaviour may give the impression of over-confidence and self-assuredness, but can be a veil for insecurity and a poor self-regard.

When you act in a submissive or non-assertive way, you use a lot of nervous energy by worrying about upsetting others. You can save yourself all that by being more assertive.

Making positive changes to your life will naturally increase your self-esteem and your confidence, but listed below are some examples of specific ways you can alter your behaviour in order to become more assertive.

- Use brief statements and get to the point. Avoid long rambling speeches that cause confusion. Be clear about what you want.
- Avoid justifications such as 'I wouldn't normally do this but . . .' – such statements tend to weaken your argument.
- Don't apologize profusely before you ask for something – for

example, 'I'm terribly sorry to bother you . . .' This also weakens your position. You don't need to seek permission to ask for what you want.

- Find out how your plans fit in with others by asking questions. Discover what a project involves before you agree to it.
- Give yourself time to consider requests when not under pressure. Get into the habit of saying, 'Let me think about it' or 'I'll have to check my diary'.
- Don't dismiss yourself by saying things like, 'I could do with some help with this but it's OK, I'll manage . . .' This just invites people to ignore your needs.
- Don't put yourself down by saying things like, 'I'm hopeless at this . . .' This weakens your position and is a dead giveaway for low self-esteem and lack of assertiveness.
- Avoid statements or questions that will come across as threatening or overbearing, such as, 'That's useless, it will never work' or 'Why on earth did you do that?' They come across as controlling and aggressive.
- Avoid sarcasm or 'put downs'.
- Use steady eye contact to reinforce your point. Submissive people often avoid eye contact and inadvertently give the other person control of the situation, while aggressive people tend to stare at their opponent and dominate.
- Use open body language and sit or stand in a relaxed posture with head held up. Avoid nervous movements such as hand wringing or folded arms. Submissive people tend to curl up to protect themselves, assertive people stand up and face the world, and aggressive people lean forward and attack.
- Find inventive ways around problems and obstacles.
- Above all, to behave in an assertive manner, it helps to have solid goals and a plan that you are deeply committed to and passionate about. That way, you have something to stand up for and will be far less likely to submit to the will of others.

Unrealistic expectations

When people plan the perfect life, understandably they expect it to be perfect. Unfortunately, perfection is just an illusion. The road to our dreams sometimes winds in unforeseen ways. That's exciting! We can't possibly plan for everything or know what we want so completely that there is no room for new developments, new tangents. We have to remain unattached to the outcome and open to opportunities we could never have planned for. When we have expectations, we often want things to be predictable, to be perfectly as we imagined them to be. But it's the imperfections that make life interesting. Isn't it the little quirks about people that we love, not the fact that they are perfect? Don't we enjoy parties more when they are spontaneous? Don't you just love gifts when they are unexpected? The point here is that the perfect life we plan sometimes works out so much better when life throws in her own twists and turns. The way things work out sometimes makes them unique in ways we could never have planned or prepared for.

People sometimes expect too much of themselves. In this hectic modern life, people may expect to balance a demanding job, an exhausting round of social engagements, a contented family and a million other things as well. Often, it's a good recipe for a heart attack or stroke! We have to learn to decipher what we really want, and what is just 'stuff to do' in our lives. We can spend an inordinate amount of time attending to the petty details of existence and end up feeling used up and burned out. I've come across many people who learn the hard way that you can't be all things to all people even for *some* of the time, and that it really doesn't matter if the windows stay dirty for another week, that someone has left the top off the toothpaste, or that you didn't make it to the 'social event of the year'. Much of it simply comes down to good time management, and we will be looking at this in detail later.

There are so many excuses for not changing your life, but think for a moment of the consequences of not doing so . . .

To strike a sombre note, time slips away so quickly, and before you know it there may not be enough of your life left to do the things you dreamed of. There is only an emptiness, and sadness for what might have been. I worked as a nurse in a hospice for several years and have cared for dying patients throughout my nursing career. I will always remember the sadness and frustration when people's hopes and aspirations were cut short by terminal illness and the regret for all the things they had never achieved because they didn't get around to it. Many times, dying patients would say to me, 'Do what makes you happy, you just don't know how long you have left.' I have heard the same from people who have been disabled and have had their dreams crushed by life's tragedies.

In truth, none of us know when we'll die or have our life turned upside down by some tragic accident or illness. Cherish each day as if it were your last day on Earth, because one day it will be. Life, all life, is fragile – and should never be taken for granted. I feel very privileged to have had such insight into the thoughts and emotions of people experiencing these profound transformations. The lesson here is to prioritize and focus on what is important. This book will help you find your true path and avoid the regrets so many have. Your life is precious. You are a unique and special person with a purpose only you can fulfil. Don't die, like so many do, without reaching your full potential and realizing your dreams.

Life's lessons and adversity

Imagine a world where we all had exactly what we want whenever we wanted it, with no price to pay. The world would descend into chaos! No one would value what they had since they didn't earn it, and life would become very dreary and predictable with no challenges and nothing to work towards. We need adversity to balance success. Everything has its place on a continuum of opposites, good and evil, big and small, happy and sad, strong and weak, light and dark. How can you know one without knowing the other? In Hawaii there is a saying, 'No rain, no rainbows', while the Chinese symbol for adversity is the same one as for opportunity. If we choose to look for the lessons in the hard times, our lives will be so much richer. In every adversity there is an opportunity to learn and grow and take a better path. Failure, as we have seen, is simply a mechanism whereby we learn to get it right. We move along the continuum towards success with every attempt, but people who don't try again after failing once never use this opportunity – and consequently 'never get there'.

Just think of people you know and about events in your own life. Sometimes the things we believe are totally devastating and the end of the world at the time turn out to be the best thing that could have happened. The greater the adversity – the greater the seed of opportunity.

When I suffered a back injury in the early 1990s I was forced to give up my nursing career. I loved nursing, yet being forced to re-evaluate my life opened up so many wonderful opportunities. I started a small business and began to study with the Open University, which became a revelation for me having never considered the possibility that I actually had the ability to study to degree level. I loved studying as much as I loved nursing, and I went on to study marine biology full time at a conventional university, graduating just after my fortieth birthday. As I write this, I'm working towards a PhD, and I would never have considered the idea in a zillion years had it not been for that devastating blow that made me change my life. I gained so much and have even continued part time with my nursing, since I simply couldn't bear to give it up completely. I love it more than ever now, and truly appreciate it.

Life prods us all the time to change direction or learn to get it right. If we don't get the message, we suffer harder and harder prods until we do finally get it. How often do you bash your head against a brick wall with something, never making any headway and coming up against bigger and ever more fearsome obstacles until you try a different approach or do something completely different, or even give up on it, and then suddenly everything falls into place? If you don't get it with a couple of prods, you will when the roof finally falls in on your head! Learn to evaluate things as you go along and look for the lesson in everything that happens.

The more adversity we endure and the more lessons we learn from adversity, the easier we can recognize it when it – as it inevitably will – comes round again. With experience, we come to know that adversity is nothing to fear, and that often it will bring the most wonderful changes to our lives, including new-found wisdom and strength.

6

Getting your mind to identify your goals

To achieve something, you have to really want it. Desire is the oomph that keeps you going when things get tough and gives you the motivation you need to achieve success. If you are not sure about something, it is easy to let it slip away. You need to have a longing that has to be satisfied. You have to have passion. When you have a burning desire, nothing can pull you away from your dream. What gets you excited? What do you feel passionate about?

Also, in order to make things happen, you need to control your enthusiasm and focus it where it is needed – to achieve your planned goals. Uncontrolled enthusiasm can dissipate your energy and get 'spent' on the wrong things. Focus your burning desire on achieving your planned goals and nothing will stand in your way.

There are a number of ways of getting your mind to come up with your true goals. This chapter focuses on how to be true to yourself, and looks at practical ways to find out what your dream is.

Let's start with a short, simple and effective exercise. Just imagine for a moment that you've won the lottery. What would you do if you had a million pounds? Would that make a difference to your life? Take a piece of paper and make a list of all the things you'd do with the money, if you haven't already done this at some point! Would you move house, change your job, start your own business, travel? Think about this for a few minutes and take the time to write all your answers down, quickly, without thinking about it too much.

Hopefully that's jolted your brain into some new activity! Next we'll refine this, and look at your list again.

Other exercises we're going to look at include:

- how to focus;
- evaluating others;
- how to clarify your principles;
- how to persist;
- finding your strengths and weaknesses;
- ways of trusting your intuition.

How to focus

Go back to your list again. Spend plenty of time writing it and include anything that comes to mind, no matter how daft it sounds. No one is going to see it, it's *your* list, so feel free to brainstorm and get it all out on paper. Write down all the things you would love to do, but don't feel capable of. Maybe you have always wanted to become a doctor, but couldn't see yourself studying to that level. Write it on the list and leave nothing out!

When you have done this, refine it further by drawing up a shortlist. What would you do if you only had six months to live? Try to really imagine that a doctor has told you that you have a terminal illness and that there is nothing that can be done to treat it. Feel the emotion and get in touch with your passion about the things you would want to do. Make it real. Now go through the list again and put a red star next to the things you would definitely want to do, or have in your life, if you had only six months to live. Write out this shortlist again on another piece of paper, because these are the things that are most important to you. The rest of the list is nice, but not vital. Keep that list for later.

Now take another piece of paper and draw a line down the middle. On one side put the heading 'Things I have to do', and on the other side 'Things I'd like to do'. Now under the 'Things I have to do', write down the things on your shortlist that are the most important to you. Again no one will see the list, so don't feel inhibited; just prioritize everything and decide on the things that you simply have to do, or have, in your life. Put down all the things that have the most meaning for you, and that would leave a big hole in your life if you didn't get to achieve them. Now put the other things on the 'Things I'd like to do' side of the page, leaving out anything that has since become unimportant and that can go on the original list. These things would be nice, but you wouldn't be devastated if you didn't achieve or have them. How do you feel about these things? What excites you?

Now you have a better idea of what is important in your life, but we can refine this even more. If you want to do what you love most in life, think about what makes you really lose track of time and what you get totally absorbed in more than anything else. This is a sign of your true desires and your true purpose. With all the money in the world, you won't have a sense of fulfilment and purpose unless you are truly following your heart and doing something that is important and worthwhile to you (not to anybody else!). People spend years working to accumulate great wealth and have every material possession they could possibly wish for, and yet remain empty and unsatisfied. *You* are not going to waste years like that – you're going to find your heartfelt dream and live it now!

So now take another piece of paper and write down all the things that really absorb you. Things where time means nothing and you get completely lost in the moment. Is it writing, painting, reading, studying, walking in nature? Just write it all down as a list, then go through the list as before with a red pen, putting a star next to all the things that are most important and which, if you had a short time left on this earth, you would simply have to make time for, whatever. It could be one or two things, it could be all of them, it doesn't matter. By now, you should have a better idea of what is important to you.

Still stumped? Why not make another list of all the things you would like to try – rally driving, skiing, watercolour painting, meditation, studying languages, gardening . . . you never know what will grab your interest until you try it. You might fancy something that turns out to be a complete disappointment when you actually try it, but it is fun to have a go at different things and you get to meet lots of new and interesting people. We are so fortunate to be living in these times when there is so much choice; it's a sacrilege to waste such wonderful opportunities, so get out there and have a go. You could find just that 'something' that has been missing in your life and that could turn into your unique dream.

Keep your lists and consider them over the next few days. You may want to revise them and contemplate them further. The next part of finding your true self and your dream life is to find your principles and values – 'your true north'. To find genuine purpose and fulfilment in life, your dreams have to be in alignment with your principles and values.

The importance of focus

Think about your lists and what is dearest to you. What you think about predominantly you can become, as your brain develops new neural pathways. You are today the sum total of what you have thought about in the past. What you focus on becomes your reality. This is why unhappy people stay miserable – they focus on their misery. The great bit, of course, is that you have complete control over your thoughts. You can choose to change the thoughts you have, and instead focus them on your dreams, and thereby change your whole life.

Evaluating others

We are attracted to other people by a deep connection: a similarity in our character and our inner values. It is that indefinable 'something' called chemistry, both the sexual and non-sexual chemistry that attracts us to the people in our life. We recognize something of ourselves in others at a very basic level. Because of this we can discover quite a lot about ourselves from the people we like and admire, so as another exercise take a piece of paper and make a list of all the people, living or dead, who inspire you. Who do you admire, respect, love, and wish to emulate? What is it about them you find fascinating? Again, this is your list. Don't feel obliged out of politeness to include people you think should be on the list! No one will read it but you.

Now, with the red pen, mark those you find most inspiring and try to think why. Make some notes against each name as you go along. You might want to imagine you were giving a small dinner party, say for about six people. Who would you invite from the list, regardless of whether or not they would get on together! This gives you a much better idea of the qualities you recognize in yourself or wish to develop in your own character.

Next draw up another list of all the people you hate or dislike and write down why. 'Go for it' and really have it out with them – they will never see the list! Again, take the red pen and mark those people who are most hateful to you. It can be quite a liberating exercise, but can also give you a better idea of yourself, since what you hate in others, you fear you have in yourself. We all have good and bad qualities and degrees of all the character traits. It is a continuum on to which we fit somewhere along the scale. Be aware of what you dislike in others and why.

How to clarify your principles

Principles form your ultimate belief system from which your values emerge. Your attitude to life and the way you treat yourself and others is shaped by your main beliefs. The basis of character is being responsible for your own actions. The way we know whether we are acting in alignment with our principles is through our conscience. Conscience is self-awareness, and understanding of your true self.

Align your principles with your conscience and free will. Notice when you feel uncomfortable with something that is not right for you. When you have a solid set of principles and values that you live by every day, the agony of making correct decisions disappears. You will always be guided to make the right decision for you. Don't mistake cultural values for authentic values. What society or other people have decreed as enlightened values may not be true for you. Take time to consider what is important to you, then be true to yourself and don't worry about appearing silly or unreasonable. In trying to fool others, we only fool ourselves.

Make a list of principles that are important to you. No one can choose them for you; you have to grow and develop into them as you begin to love your life and live your dream. Remember that principles and values are not the same thing. Principles form the basic foundation of who you are, and are determined by your conscience, your 'true north'. When your values are aligned with your principles you experience peace, harmony and happiness. For example, you may believe in the principle of karma – in other words, that you reap what you sow. Your values, therefore, will be determined by this principle, and an example may include treating people with compassion and kindness.

Your conscience will be different from someone else's. It is not right or wrong, just different. When we act against our conscience, there is conflict. This is the cause of inner turmoil and emotional discomfort, which blocks our progress. It is not productive in personal or business relationships with others or in the attainment of your goals and aspirations. Develop self-awareness and look for signs of conflict. Notice your feelings and reactions to the people and things in your life. When you are trying to please others against your principles and values, you are not being true to yourself. Listen to your intuition, your inner awareness of your true nature, and watch for the physical signs in your body that warn you of conflicting reactions – the forced smiles and uncomfortable feelings when interacting with others. When there is no conflict of conscience, you feel harmony and are able to trust yourself and others.

In relation to this point, it is worth exploring some character traits (not a definitive list, by any means!) and the implications they may have on your life:

Honesty

Being honest with yourself is fundamental to getting anywhere in life, otherwise you end up going round in circles, never really knowing what you want. We are very good at deceiving ourselves into believing anything that serves our immediate purpose – whether we believe it or not on a conscious level. We have already seen how past conditioning can influence us and how we can become entrenched in faulty thinking. Only by knowing who you really are can you accept yourself, love yourself, and then begin to change things and become the person you want to be. Self-honesty is very empowering. By being honest with yourself, you develop self-respect, earn the respect of others, and discover the freedom to be yourself.

Honesty with others comes from being honest with yourself. Life is an illusion without honesty. Being honest with people shows you respect them and respect yourself. Being honest saves getting tied up in knots trying to remember what you said; it saves time and effort and is basically a much simpler way to deal with people! We appreciate people who tell it like it is with tact and honesty; it saves precious time and allows us to make decisions based on the truth. It is emotional openness and being genuine with people. Would you rather know what someone really feels or be told what they think you want to hear? When people are honest with us we learn to trust them. Building genuine and loving relationships with others depends on honesty and trust. Without honesty, nothing is real.

Integrity

Wisdom is knowing what you should do. Integrity is doing it. Our conscience and our guiding principles show us the right thing to do, and when we act with integrity we follow what is in our heart – we do the right thing. Sometimes we do not have the wisdom or experience to know what is right. Many times there is no right answer, but if we do the very best we can and follow our conscience, then we still act with integrity. If we have made a mistake, we can learn from it and do better next time, it is part of being human. Conflicts arise when we know what we should do, but we ignore or act against our intuition or inner voice.

Courage

Courage is having the nerve to put your dreams above your fears and facing what has to be done, whether it is scaling a mountain or simply saying sorry. It is being able to look deeply inside yourself to discover who you are and to keep trying when you fail. Courage is being able to take the next step in making your life better. Take a deep breath, 'feel the fear, and do it anyway'. You will develop strength and maturity as you face your fears and overcome them, but be realistic too. Evaluate the dangers and consequences before you act. Having courage will help enormously in your quest to find and live your dream.

Independence

Being independent means refusing to be controlled or manipulated by anyone. It means having the self-respect to stand by your principles and your decisions and the courage to be who you are and to live the life you want, even in the face of opposition. Being independent frees you of the need for other people. You may choose to be with others, but you don't need them to lean on or make decisions for you; you have the strength to be alone if you choose. We come into this world alone and we leave alone. We alone are answerable for the life we choose to live, yet so many define themselves through other people – their spouses, their children, their heroes – that they lose themselves and their own unique purpose in the process. People become so dependent on others that they are unable to function alone. Many people can't even bear to be alone for more than a few minutes. Nothing is for ever and the one thing you can rely on in life is that things change – circumstances, people, the environment we live in. Your inner strength and sense of independence will help see you through the problems and challenges of life. Seek time to be alone every day and to contemplate your goals and direction in life. We often make ourselves too busy with daily 'stuff to do' and coping with the demands of other people to do the most important thing of all – to be still and listen with our intuition to our own true inner being.

Positive mental attitude

A positive attitude influences your whole life, determining thoughts and feelings, conversations, actions, goals and direction. A positive attitude can open up many possibilities, just as a negative attitude may shut them out.

A positive attitude starts with our thoughts. As we discovered, we have complete and absolute control over what we think and we can consciously choose to think positive thoughts and rewire our brain with new neural networks for success.

Some people seem lucky enough to be born with a positive attitude, but others have to work at it. No matter what you came into this world with, you have the ability to develop a positive state of mind – one positive thought at a time. Every time a negative thought comes into your mind, immediately stop, and turn it into a positive one. Consider the positive, negative and neutral outcomes in order to build a sense of balanced expectations. It might take practice and persistence, but it works, and will start to bring many positive changes into your life. Relationships will improve, problems turn into challenges, and hope and enthusiasm will grow. You begin to see opportunities where negative clouds previously obscured your vision of the future. You begin to believe that you really can make your dreams come true and make positive plans to make it happen.

Once you start this, you eventually begin to feel uncomfortable around negative people and tend to avoid them. In fact, I highly recommend that you *do* avoid negative, cynical people who try to dampen your enthusiasm or control you with their unproductive and negative approach, which will do nothing to bring them success in life. Concentrate fully on becoming positive and optimistic. You can achieve whatever you believe in wholeheartedly. Don't let anyone stop you or trample on your dreams. No one has a right to do that.

High self-esteem

When you have taken an honest look at who you are and worked on the areas you are not happy about, you will see an increase in your self-esteem. You will start to like yourself and have more self-respect. High self-esteem means you will not allow others to mistreat you and that you value yourself, your time, your dreams and your life. Healthy self-esteem is good to develop if you want to love your life, live your dreams and find happiness.

How to persist

Even with a burning desire to achieve your goals, it is too easy to give up at the first obstacle or quit because it is all taking too long. You need persistence to stay on track and belief that your efforts will be rewarded when the time is right.

When you centre your life on your principles, you create a solid foundation you can depend on. This has been proven to be true over thousands of years of human history. From your 'centre', you have personal power and freedom and are not undermined by external circumstances. You create self-trust, and when you trust yourself, you do not rely on others or on external events. When you have inner strength and integrity, you maintain your dignity as a human being.

But how can you make the right choices when you don't have a clear idea of what your values are, or without knowing what will fulfil your deepest physical, emotional, spiritual and intellectual needs?

Finding your strengths and weaknesses

Strengths, weaknesses, opportunities, threats (SWOT)

Companies often use a form of SWOT analysis to analyse their business, and there is no reason why you can't use this approach in your personal life too. It is always useful to summarize and focus.

What are your strengths and weaknesses, what opportunities do you see developing for you, and what are the threats you might face?

Strengths might include things like your talents, abilities and skills or character traits such as persistence or integrity.

Weaknesses might include a deficit in your knowledge (which you can rectify by learning what you need to know) or a lack of finance for a project.

Opportunities might include things like the possibility of working with others to achieve your aims, a positive outcome following a redundancy, or a new opportunity in an area you had not previously considered. There are opportunities around us all the time if we have the heart to look for them.

Threats include all the things you fear, real or perceived. You might consider things such as illnesses or accidents and financial setbacks as threats, but in truth, when you are focused on your goals, there is little that can threaten your success. No one can lead you away from your chosen path when you are committed to making your dreams come true.

What are the experiences that have shaped your life the most? What have you learned from these experiences? Think about the dreams you want to achieve. How do you think they might shape your life in the future and while you strive to achieve them?

How would you want your epitaph to read? How would you want people to remember you? Sum it up in just a few sentences and write it down. It is a useful exercise in discovering what you want your life to be about and what you would like to be remembered for. Do it now – it's too late when you are on your death bed!

Now you should have all the information you need to put together a mission statement for your life. A mission statement is a couple of sentences to sum up what your life is about. What is your mission in life? Write it down and keep it handy. Refer to it often to keep you focused and let it act as a framework for your goals. We all need a mission in life – something that's important to us and that we are willing to work for and fight for. If you don't stand for something, you'll fall for anything. What is it that you stand for?

Think big

When you start setting goals for yourself you will probably start with small, easily achievable goals to give you confidence and belief in yourself while you adapt to a new way of thinking. However, you also have to challenge yourself. Go for the biggest dream you want – it's better to aim for the stars and end up on the moon than never reach for the sky! If you want to be the best, don't settle for mediocre – just go for it!

The aim is to stretch yourself while remaining realistic. If you want to be an astronaut and you have a morbid fear of heights, you know that you have a lot of work ahead! You can achieve impossible dreams by being realistic, and by breaking your dream up into manageable chunks. You can eat an elephant one bite at a time, and you can achieve your big dream one thought and one step at a time. Even if you don't have all the necessary skills now, you can gain the skills, training and knowledge you need to achieve your dream life. There are so many opportunities to learn, via the local library, colleges, universities and the internet.

To think big, maintain an overall vision of where you are going. It is easy to lose direction when you get bogged down with day-to-day life. This is why you need to refer back to your lists and your mission statement. Keep them in a file and look at them regularly for inspiration and to keep you focused on the horizon.

Ways of trusting your intuition

Deep down, you already know what is right for you and which direction you should take – you just have to consciously access the information. Learn to trust yourself. Listen to your inner voice, your intuition. It is your best friend and is almost never wrong if you take the time to listen. Deep down, we know what is in our hearts and we know what is best for us in any given situation. We just have to learn to recognize the signals that our bodies are sending us.

Usually intuition warns you not to do something. It's a gut feeling that something is not quite right. How often, when things have gone wrong, have you said, 'If only I'd listened to my gut feeling' or 'I just *knew* it was the wrong thing to do, I should have known better'. We often rely on our logical minds when we really should listen to the small voice inside us, which is aligned with our principles and will always do what is right for us.

How often have you heard the phone ring and just 'knew' who it would be, or thought about someone you haven't seen in ages and then bumped into them in the supermarket? And how often has your intuition prompted you to do something that turned out to be a fabulous opportunity, or started off a series of coincidences that led to worthwhile changes in your life?

The left hemisphere of our brain is the logical side, responsible for words, numbers, sequences, analysis and lists. The right hemisphere is where intuition originates and is involved in rhythm, spatial awareness, imagination, daydreaming, colour and dimension. The left hemisphere is the dominant side of our brain, and the right side often becomes weak because we don't use it often enough. We all have intuition or gut feelings about things, yet often it is difficult to recognize this as our heads are full of instructions from other people. Many of them are negative and detrimental to us, yet have become embroiled in our minds and indistinguishable from our own true feelings. We need to learn to stop and listen to our own inner voice,

73

clear of all the clutter. You have to just 'be' for a while. You could call it meditation, but it is essentially just stopping the noise in your head in order to get in touch with your true self. It is getting into the gap between your thoughts.

It is not always easy at first since we're not used to listening to our 'inner guide', but it does get less hard with practice. If you have decisions to make and are not sure what to do or can't decide what direction to take, think it through and consider all your options, then turn it over to your subconscious mind and listen to your intuition. It will almost invariably be right. Sometimes we can go round in circles with reasoning and tie ourselves up in knots trying to work things out logically. Try simply trusting your gut instincts.

Find some space in your day to be alone – a special place where you won't be disturbed by anyone or anything. Just take some time every day to quietly sit alone, close your eyes, and silence your mind. As you sit peacefully, think of black velvet or concentrate your thoughts on a candle flame. Just 'be'. When fleeting thoughts come into your mind, just let them pass and renew your concentration on nothingness. After around 20 minutes or so you may start to get a feeling about something, which is your intuition starting to guide you. Sometimes you will get answers very clearly. The more you practise, the more you will recognize your intuition. Learn to notice the feelings you get in your body in response to people, situations or your own thoughts. You may feel a warning knot in your stomach or a 'hunch' about something. If you do get answers, you should act on them immediately. Intuition is definitely time-related, and we get feelings about things only as we need them. How often have you said, 'If only I'd done that when I first thought of it; now it's too late'?

All great thinkers spend time alone in contemplation and listen to their intuition. Get into the habit of listening to your 'inner guide' and learn to trust your gut feelings. As you practise and prove that your intuition was right, you will come to rely on it more and more as a compass to your 'true north' and a guide to making decisions in your life.

7
Discover your personal thinking style

The way you process information and perceive the world around you is highly subjective and personal. It is based on the sum total of your experience to date, including the period before you were born. Much has been discovered about personal thinking styles through fields ranging from psychology to management training and education. The way we learn new information is a key to understanding our thinking or cognitive style, and researchers generally agree that there are two major categories – the way we perceive information (the sensory modality we operate in), and the way we organize and process that information through our cognitive style (the dominant side of our brain).

Learn how you perceive and process information in order to maximize the success of your goals and action plans and to detect the thinking processes of other people in your life to increase your rapport and communication with them.

Your modality

Researchers and teachers have come to realize that different pupils have optimum ways of absorbing new information and have different learning styles. Rita Dunn, a pioneer in the field of learning styles, has identified many of the variables that affect learning, including environmental, emotional, physical and sociological factors. Things like light conditions, background sound, the way you organize your work, and whether you work alone or with others can all affect your learning outcome. These variables are linked to the sensory modality that we operate through.

Your modality is the way you perceive information most easily and which sense you prefer to use. Once you are aware of this, it can help you to learn faster and more easily and help you to develop ways to support changes in your behaviour and your life by working with your brain instead of struggling against your individual thinking style. It can also help you to build rapport and communicate more effectively with others if you can identify their personal modality. John Grinder, a linguist, and Richard Bandler, a mathematician, psychotherapist and computer expert, developed *neurolinguistic programming (NLP)* in the 1970s as a means of helping people to achieve success in their lives. It is concerned with the effect of our thinking processes on our behaviour and includes the sensory modalities we use to perceive the world.

There are three basic modalities:

1 visual – seeing
2 auditory – hearing
3 kinesthetic – feeling, doing and movement

We all have a preference for one or two of these modalities, even though we use them all. Some people perceive the world primarily through sight and visual perception, others through listening and hearing, and yet others through movement and doing. Sometimes our primary modality is so strong that we have difficulty processing information through the other modalities, making all the difference between success and failure.

There are clues to deciphering your modality and that of other people. Listen carefully to your speech. If you are a visual person you may catch yourself saying things like, 'That looks good' or 'OK, I get the picture'. If you are an auditory person, you may say, 'That sounds great' or 'That rings a bell'. A kinesthetic person would say, 'That feels right' or 'I'll be in touch'.

Other clues can be found in how you tackle a physical task such as putting together a self-assembly bookcase. People with a primary visual modality would first read the instructions to understand how to put it together; auditory people would prefer to get someone to tell them how to do it; and kinesthetic people would prefer to start working with the parts in order to find out how it fits together.

The words we use in speech are process words. When we perceive something in our mind it is processed via our sensory modality and the words we use reflect that modality. We can create rapport with people by matching their modality. For example, if you are a kinesthetic person and you are talking to a visual person, stand up or sit up straight – it will help you to speak faster to match their pace. You can also strengthen your communication by using visual props such as handouts, photos, etc. On the other hand, if you are talking to a kinesthetic person, relax, lean back and slow your pace to match theirs. Using this and other body-language-matching techniques helps to create rapport.

The way you behave also gives clues as to your primary modality. Some people have a strong primary and a secondary modality while others can operate comfortably in all three. There is usually a preference for one or two modalities, though. Which do you recognize in yourself and others?

Visual people

- Neat and orderly.
- Speak quickly.
- Observant.
- Have a better memory for faces than names.
- Place importance on appearance.
- Are not distracted by noise.
- Have trouble remembering verbal instructions. Prefer them to be written down.
- Like art more than music.
- Would rather do a demonstration than make a speech.
- Would rather read than be read to and are fast readers.
- Doodle during conversations.

Auditory people

- Talk to themselves a lot.
- Are easily distracted by noise.
- Can spell better out loud than in writing.
- Like music more than art.
- Are talkative, love chatting and spend time in lengthy descriptions.
- Find writing difficult, but are better at talking when explaining something.
- Have problems with visualization.
- Like reading aloud and listening to stories.
- Are eloquent speakers.

Kinesthetic people

- Move around a lot and can't sit still.
- Pace about when talking on the phone.
- Learn by doing things.

- Gesture a lot.
- Use action words.
- Think better when walking.
- Have trouble with geography unless they have been to a place.
- Respond to physical rewards.
- Speak slowly.
- Stand close to people and touch them to get their attention.
- May have messy handwriting.
- Like plot-oriented books.

Clues to a person's modality can be found in their body language, but our thinking preference is also apparent in our eye movements. This is because we access different parts of the brain when we are thinking, and this is called 'eye accessing cues' in NLP.

- *Visually created images.* When we imagine something or visualize something that we have constructed in our mind, we tend to look upward and to the right.
- *Visually remembered images.* When we remember something we have seen, we tend to look up and to the left.
- *Created sounds.* When we imagine sounds, such as when we make up tunes, we tend to look to the right, but not up or down.
- *Remembered sounds.* When we remember a sound we've heard, we tend to look to the left but not up or down.
- *Feelings and bodily sensations.* When we tune in to our feelings and bodily sensations, we tend to look down and to the right.
- *Internal dialogue.* When we are conducting an internal conversation with ourselves, we tend to look down and to the left.

Even when you are aware of this, it is difficult to catch yourself following the patterns, so watch out for them in other people who are not aware that you are watching out for them. Ask someone to remember something they saw, and they should look up and to their left. Ask them to get in touch with how they are feeling, and they should look down and to their right. The movements can be very fast and fleeting, especially with visual stimuli.

What's your thinking style?

The modality is the way we perceive information, but how we process information involves brain dominance – in other words, whether we predominantly favour the right or left side of the brain. Each hemisphere of the brain specializes in certain skills and modes of thinking, although there is some crossover. As we noted earlier, the left-brain thinking processes are sequential, logical, linear and rational. It is the side of the brain that is highly organized and is involved in verbal expression, writing, reading, auditory association symbolism and finding out details and facts. The right-brain thinking processes are random, intuitive and abstract. It is the side of the brain that is involved in feelings, intuition, spatial awareness, shape and pattern recognition, art, music, creativity and visualization. The ideal is to use both sides of your brain in a balanced way for success in all aspects of life. However, society favours left-brain thinking, which can lead to imbalance and poor mental and physical health if you do not make an effort to include some right-brain activities. If you tend to be logical and orderly in your approach, for example, try taking up a creative hobby such as drawing, dancing, acting or learning a musical instrument to give your whole brain a workout.

Whatever thinking style predominates, it helps to find support from others who value your thinking style as this will reinforce the positive aspects for you. Also by understanding the way others think, you can work and communicate more effectively with them. For instance, don't try to communicate too much detail or too many rules and regulations to a highly creative, abstract thinker, as this will be counterproductive. Try giving general ideas and maintain a friendly, open atmosphere.

Take the test in Table 1 (overleaf) to see if you are a left- or a right-brain thinker.

Table 1

Read each set of words or statements and circle the one from each question that best describes you. There are no right or wrong answers; just be as honest as you can.

Question 1	*Question 6*
A Reading/studying	A Factual
B Warm	B Arts
Question 2	*Question 7*
A Imaginative	A Untidy
B Analytical	B Organized
Question 3	*Question 8*
A Sensitive	A Numbers
B Precise	B Thinking
Question 4	*Question 9*
A Feeling	A Creative
B Speaking	B Cool
Question 5	*Question 10*
A Science	A Competitive
B Intuition	B Spontaneous

Now, in the grid in Table 2, add up your score by circling the letters (A or B) of the words you chose for each question. Add up the number of letters you have circled for each column. The highest scores indicate the way you most frequently process information: left-brained and logical, or right-brained and creative. Some people are fairly evenly balanced, but most will favour one style more than the other.

Table 2

Question	Column one	Column two
1	A	B
2	B	A
3	B	A
4	B	A
5	A	B
6	A	B
7	B	A
8	A	B
9	B	A
10	A	B
Total		

Column one: If you have a higher total in column one, you are predominantly a left-brain thinker: organized, logical and analytical.

Column two: If you have a higher total in column two, you are predominantly a right-brain thinker: random, creative and intuitive.

Table 3

To develop your left brain (if you had a low score in column one)	To develop your right brain (if you had a low score in column two)
Keep a diary of your daily activities and organize your week	Keep a diary of your feelings
Read newspapers and factual books	Write a short story and read more fiction
Put together a speech or presentation on your favourite subject	Learn to paint and draw
Organize your finances on a computer spreadsheet	Make something with clay
Make a list of items you need in order to redecorate a room, or a list of plants you would put in the garden	Redesign a room in your house or your garden
Make a 'Mind Map' of your goals and plans and list ways you would achieve them	Make a 'Mind Map' of your feelings about your life and how you would feel if you changed things
Write a list of all the new experiences in life you want to try out	Write a story about yourself and your life and what you want to achieve
Go to the library and explore the internet to find out as much as you can about an interesting new hobby	Visualize yourself doing something new and exciting
Write plans and lists of things to do every day	Daydream more often

The more uneven your score in Table 2, the more you need to work on your lower scoring thinking style in order to balance your brain power.

Table 3 gives you some ideas of things you can do to boost your left- or right-thinking style.

The main thing is to be aware of your predominant thinking style and try to balance your activities to get the opposite side of your brain working too. For example, if you sit at a desk all day using the left side of your brain, try to get out for a walk in the country and allow yourself to daydream and engage the right side to balance your thinking process. You will find that by achieving more balance, you will think more efficiently and be able to make improvements to your life in many ways. The following case history illustrates how this awareness can make all the difference between success and failure.

Charlotte

Charlotte was a right-brain thinker and very creative in her work and personal life, but she discovered problems with her thinking style when she started her own business as a wedding planner. She loved coming up with ideas for her customers and planning elaborate weddings for them, and this was her strength in the business. However, Charlotte consistently failed to follow through on the detail and became disheartened with all the organizational tasks that had to be done in order to make a wedding actually happen for her customers. She hated the phone calls, ordering from suppliers, dealing with the day-to-day running of the business, and was always running out of time for getting things done. She was worried that her business was suffering and felt a failure personally because she couldn't cope.

When Charlotte realized how she processed information predominantly using her right brain, she decided to tackle the immediate problem by taking on an assistant who had a more logical, ordered style of thinking, who thrived on the organizational tasks and was able to attend to the details that Charlotte hated. Once Charlotte was free to work with her creative thinking style, knowing her assistant would follow through with the organizational details, Charlotte's business became a huge success, attracting customers who valued her ideas and vision. Charlotte began to feel more positive about herself and stopped feeling guilty. She realized that her thinking style was unique, and was the basis of her business success provided she recognized that she needed help with the organization and the details. She even began to work with her assistant to learn how to develop her left-brain thinking processes and become more balanced in her approach.

'Mind Mapping' – working with your brain

It was traditionally thought that the brain processed information in a structured, linear form because this is how we speak and write, but recent research has discovered that this is just the result of our thinking style. The actual process of thinking is rather different, and the brain must sort out a jumble of random ideas, words, feelings, sounds, symbols, images and associations and simultaneously order them into a coherent format. This creates a burst of electrical activity that radiates outwards and spreads across the whole brain as it travels through the neural networks associated with the thoughts we are thinking at the time. This radiant thinking pattern inspired Tony Buzan in the early 1970s to create a method of expressing our thoughts on paper that he called 'Mind Mapping'.

A 'Mind Map' is a two-dimensional representation of the multi-dimensional way our brains think, encompassing space, time and colour. The subject of the Mind Map is put in the centre of the page as an image, with the main themes radiating outwards as branches from the central image. A key word is printed on the line of these branches and they open out into a network of finer branches with associated words and images, much like a neural network would work in the brain. A Mind Map is enhanced with colour, pictures and symbols to personalize them, reinforce associations and improve recall, and can be used for many different things – particularly learning and planning your life and your goals. Mind Mapping is a way of working with the way your brain processes information instead of struggling with traditional linear forms of note-taking and planning.

Figure 6 shows a Mind Map of *The Thinking Person's Guide To Happiness*, to give you an idea of how it all works.

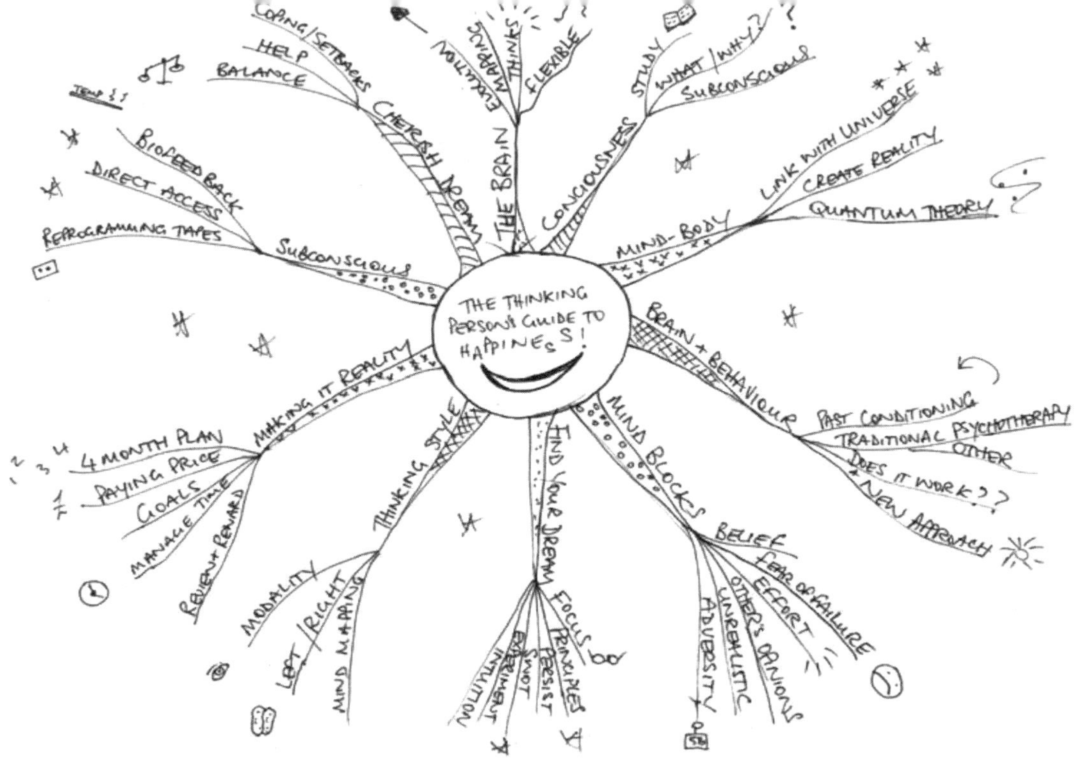

Figure 6 A Mind Map

To make a Mind Map, start in the middle of a large piece of paper turned sideways and use coloured pens, one for each branch of the Mind Map. Write your main idea in the middle and enclose it with a shape such as a circle or cloud or illustrate it. Place branches radiating outwards from your main idea and use each branch to print a key idea or association. Make important ideas larger and more prominent. Finer branches should radiate outwards from the main branches with further details and associations, also printed for clarity. Use colour liberally and have one colour for each key idea. Illustrate your Mind Map with photos and images, symbols and arrows. Be outrageous and creative so that you will remember it. Mind Maps are useful for seeing the big picture and to view different aspects of a subject simultaneously because we often get bogged down in the details. Try making some Mind Maps to prove to yourself how effective they can be.

You can use Mind Mapping to help create new neural networks and depress old, unwanted pathways. Think of a specific problem in your life such as a behaviour you want to change. Now draw a Mind Map that concentrates on the old associations with the behaviour, asking questions such as: 'Why do I behave in a certain way?', 'How do I feel about it?', 'What is stopping me from changing?' and 'What are the consequences of my not changing?' Draw this Mind Map in black and white only and don't use too many symbols. In other words, make it rather dull and dreary. Call the Mind Map 'old'.

Next draw a Mind Map that focuses on the new behaviour you want to develop and challenges your old beliefs. Make it bold and bright and memorable with lots of illustrations. Pose questions such as: 'What can I do to change?', 'How will I feel?', 'How will I look?', 'What will I be doing when I have changed?' Call the Mind Map 'new'.

Figures 7 and 8 are examples of two Mind Maps that Dylan drew up to help him give up smoking. His second Mind Map, which he called 'The New Me', he drew up using bright colours (although we are only able to show it in black and white here).

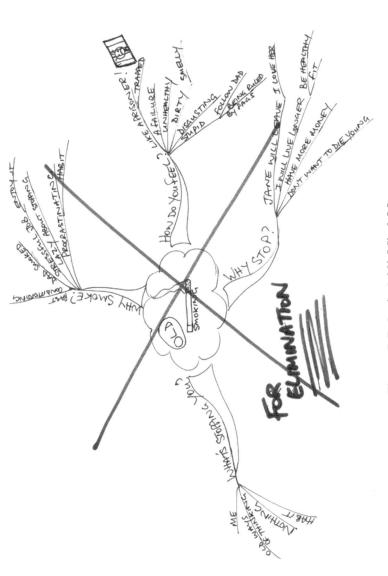

Figure 7 Dylan's 'old' Mind Map

Figure 8 Dylan's 'new' Mind Map

Review your 'old' Mind Map once or twice, then draw a big red cross through it with a thick felt-tipped pen. Put it away in an envelope marked 'OLD BELIEFS/BEHAVIOUR: FOR ELIMINA-TION'.

Now review your 'new' Mind Map once or twice, then put it in a prominent place, perhaps up on the wall where you will see it frequently. Look at it at least twice a day and add to it if you can. This will send the message to your subconscious that you are changing your behaviour, and you will find that your attitudes and beliefs will begin to change, with your subconscious supporting those changes. Also, with repetition, the new neural networks associated with the desired behaviour will begin to develop and strengthen as new synapses form between the neurons in your brain. This will reinforce your new attitudes, belief and subsequent behaviour while the old networks weaken and die away. You will be literally helping your brain to rewire itself for success.

You can also apply NLP by visualizing your new Mind Map. Try to see the Map and the ideas you have put into it as big, colourful and bright in your mind. Bring it closer and see all the details of it. Become really familiar with it in your mind's eye. Actually smile when you think of your new Mind Map and create positive associations and feelings with it. If you think about your old Mind Map, think of it and the ideas it contains as small, black and white and old and scrunched up. Don't dwell on the image, but quickly draw a large imaginary red cross over the image to very firmly send the message to your subconscious that this neural network is obsolete. Immediately go back to a bright, cheerful image of your new Mind Map and the goals and ideas you have incorporated into it. Try to create this visualization in your mind whenever you have a spare couple of minutes during the day, and particularly just before you go to sleep as this is when your mind will assimilate the information.

8

Turning thought into reality

How your mind translates 'thought' into fact

It can take several months for new ways of behaving to become permanent habits because of the length of time new neural networks in the brain take to establish themselves, mature and strengthen. Whether you are trying to get into the habit of working out at the gym or study in the evenings, you need to allow enough time for repeated actions to become habits and for your brain to establish these new neural networks. Every time you repeat an old or unwanted behaviour, you strengthen old neural networks associated with it, perpetuating your old unwanted habit, but when you repeat a new behaviour, you are strengthening the new neural networks associated with it and this will not happen overnight. This chapter looks at how to make changes in your life, including:

- specific ways of organizing your goals;
- reviews and rewards;
- managing your time – techniques that include setting time limits and eliminating 'time bandits'.

Having the courage to change

You have to believe in your dream enough to stick by it when the going gets tough. You have to have the courage to stand up and be counted, to defend your dream when others belittle you or fail to understand what it is you are trying to achieve. Keep your eyes on the horizon and know that what you are doing is right for you. Other people may have their own dreams, but many don't have a dream at all. Have the courage to be who you want to be in the face of adversity, or despite the disapproval of others. Have the determination to see it through, come what may. Be strong and independent because that is what it will take. It will feel tempting to give up at times and go back to your old ways, but never give up on something you believe with all your heart is right for you. No one else is living your unique life, experiencing your particular situation, or learning the same lessons in life as you. Only you can do it. You can't change the world and you can't change anyone in it. The only way to change your life is to change *you*.

Habits

Remember when you learned to drive a car (assuming you drive, that is!)? At first everything seemed strange and uncomfortable. You had to concentrate on working the clutch and changing gear at the same time and remembering what comes first – was it mirror, signal or manoeuvre? Yet after some practice it became second nature. Now you no longer have to think about it – your subconscious takes over and you do it automatically. It is the same with other skills, and it is the same with habits of thought. Concentrate on thinking positively. At first it may seem strange to be correcting yourself all the time, but notice when you are being negative and instantly change it to positive. For instance, catch yourself when you are out in the pouring rain. Instead of thinking how ghastly the weather is, think how wonderful it is that the rain gives us lush green fields and woodlands, and how refreshing the rain feels on our faces when we are hot. If it didn't rain, we would have no fresh water to drink or use for washing, etc. We can turn almost everything around from negative to positive and enrich our lives in the process. Use the time when you are stuck in a traffic jam to daydream or plan your goals.

The four-month plan

We will look more closely at time management in this chapter, but just for a moment, imagine if you had four months to do whatever you liked! Wouldn't it be fantastic to have four months off work, or just to do whatever you wanted to do in this period? What would you do with this time? Wouldn't it be great to have all that time to achieve your dreams?

Well, you already have it! Turn the television off! If you clocked up how many hours you spend in front of the box, you'd be amazed. Just 3 hours a night, 5 days a week, for 52 weeks of the year – that's 780 hours of television per year (and I bet most people watch more than that!). That's around 100 useful working days, 20 weeks – or around four months. In other words, you could waste four months every year in front of the telly watching rubbish (let's be honest here!). Instead of watching other people's fictional lives and hours of soaps, sport and fly-on-the-wall documentaries, why not invest the time in your own life?

I'm not suggesting that we don't watch any television at all. There are some good educational programmes, which might help us to achieve our aims, and there are times when we haven't the energy for anything other than flopping down in front of the television. We just need to be mindful of what we watch and how we spend our time.

You could reward yourself with your favourite programme once you've achieved something that will progress you towards your goal. I must admit I love hospital dramas, wildlife documentaries and the odd film, so I'll record them to watch when I have nothing better to do or when I'm too whacked to do anything else! I'll also try to catch the news headlines since I no longer buy newspapers (another 'time bandit'!). The point is to make the television part of your reward system, rather than allowing it to steal your time and stop you achieving your dreams. When you get into the habit of switching the television off without feeling deprived, you will start to value your time and use it more productively.

Paying the price

Usually, in order to make changes in our lives, we have to make room for these new things by dropping something else. In order to study in the evenings, you will definitely have to cut down on watching television and maybe give up a few social events. People moan that there is not enough time to do anything other than just get through the day, but do you know – we have the same 24 hours as Einstein and Beethoven had! The difference is they didn't squander their time, they used it for a purpose.

Evaluate what it is you want. Do you want your dream badly enough to make a few sacrifices? Achieving your goals may also mean being willing to pay the price. Are you prepared to get up an hour earlier in the morning to exercise or write another page of your book? If it's worth having, it's worth working for. The trouble is, there is no standing still. You are either gaining or slipping, either working towards something you want, or slipping away from it. You are making a choice whatever you do. Even if you do nothing, you are effectively making a choice to let it slip away while you procrastinate and try to make up your mind. Wait long enough and you lose it completely because you've run out of time or the opportunity has gone to someone else. Ultimately, you run out of life without ever having achieved your dream. So how will you spend your 24 hours a day?

Specific ways of organizing your goals

Write out your goals and your action plans. By writing them down you crystallize your thoughts and make a mental commitment to them. Writing them down forces you to be specific, and identifies the strengths and weaknesses of your plan.

Goals should include all areas of your life; some need working on and will be more prominent of course, but you should strive to balance the following aspects of your life:

- physical
- intellectual/mental
- social/relationships
- spiritual/personal growth
- financial/wealth creation
- time.

To achieve your dream, you have to break it down into manageable chunks. This is where goals and action plans come in. Each goal is a step along the path to your dream.

Be specific

State exactly what you want. If you want to change your job, write a book, achieve more freedom, move house, travel – be specific. Get as much detail as possible. Vague statements won't work, you need to be precise and really know what you want. Be concise and prioritize what it is you want. The more specific your goal statement, the easier it will be to know when it has been achieved. Being specific can also help your goals have more meaning.

A statement like 'have more freedom' or 'be less lonely' might be hard to judge. Statements like 'spend fewer hours at my job', or 'meet more new people' will be easier to evaluate.

Be realistic

If you want to lose weight or get fit, do you have a workable plan as to how you will achieve this? If you are not going to be able to attain this with your current lifestyle and commitments, how will you change things to accommodate this new goal? You won't be able to get fit overnight, but each day you can exercise a little more to get closer to your goal. Your goals have to be realistic. You really can achieve anything your heart desires, but you have to have a plan as to how you will get to your goal, one step at a time. For example, planning to lose 2 lbs over the next two weeks is easier to implement than 'losing half a stone'.

Be time-sensitive

When do you want to achieve this goal? Vague open-ended statements won't help. You have to have a deadline or otherwise your natural tendency will be to leave it and let other things take priority. Have a date by which you can realistically get there.

Being capable of change

Things change, circumstances alter our plans, for better or worse, and sometimes we simply change our minds about things. Your goals must be firm, but not set in stone. They have to be capable of changing and adapting. You might really want a new car, but while you are saving for it, you decide you want to go to college more than have the car, so your priorities change and your goal is now to save for college instead. That's OK, your plans can develop and metamorphose into much bigger or better things – and so they should. You are not a failure because you didn't achieve a particular goal. You have to build in a degree of flexibility to your plans and allow for those twists and turns that sometimes life hands out.

Plan of action

Once you have a specific, realistic, time-sensitive goal, you need a plan of action. How are you going to achieve it? Say, for example, your goal is to lose a stone in weight. How will you do it? Will you pick a diet plan, count calories, or just exercise more? Will you go to slimming classes? How long will it realistically take you to lose the weight? Have you allowed for that party next week when you won't be able to stick to your diet? Plan it out in detail and take action to achieve the various aspects. For example, you might shop for the foods you need and enrol at the local gym. Actually *do* something towards achieving your goal.

Reviews and rewards

You should evaluate your goals as you go along. Are they still valid? Are you on track? Find out if they need a 'tweak' here and there to enable you to make progress. Ideally, review your goals every day. Read them aloud and reaffirm them to yourself. Remember the habits of thought. Repeat your goals often in order to make them a real part of your life, and to strengthen new neural networks associated with them. Have them at the forefront of your mind every day. Live them fully. It is a good idea to set aside a few minutes at the same time every day to think about and repeat your goals. Write them out and put them up on the wall in a prominent place, and even go to the trouble of writing them out again every day. Make 'Mind Maps' of your goals. Your goals are the vehicle for achieving your dreams, and they have a fundamental importance in your life. Spend time on them. Most people spend more time on their shopping lists than they do planning their lives.

You should have short-term, medium-term and long-term goals. Short-term goals could be things you set yourself every day and will become part of your daily time management. Medium-term goals could be anything from six months to several years, and long-term goals could span the rest of your life. Where do you want to be in six months, a year, five years?

Look over your goals and evaluate how you are doing at least once a week. Time spent in this way will be invaluable, and could save years of blundering along on the wrong path. It will also keep you focused and inspire you to keep going if you remind yourself about what it is you are working towards. It will help you to keep your eyes on the horizon and see the bigger picture . . . see your dream unfolding.

It is a good idea to have a special file for your ongoing goals as well as your list of things you want to do, and your list of who you want to become. Make it your own private place where you are in touch with your true self, your desires, your dreams and your mission in life.

Your subconscious mind will take suggestions literally, so you must take care to impress upon it the details of what you want exactly. Hence the need for specific, time-related goals. Personal goals such as changes to your character should be made in the present tense, as if they were already happening: 'Every day I *am* becoming more and more positive, I am rejecting negative thoughts'. Your subconscious will act on this as if it is happening now, and make gradual improvements every day. There is no conflict there. If, however, it was for some vague time in the future, 'I *will* become more positive', then your subconscious will simply wait for the time to act and do nothing to help you achieve it now.

Other goals should be time-related: 'I will finish writing my book by Saturday'. Some people suggest all goals should be in the present tense, as if you had already achieved them, but to me this conflicts with the truth, so that your conscious mind will not accept and believe it enough to allow your subconscious to accept and act upon it.

Plan in some rewards along the way to keep you on track. A long soak in the bath when you've written another 1,000 words perhaps, watching that film you want to see on Saturday when you've finished your presentation for work. Rewards keep you moving towards your goals and make the whole thing more fun.

Managing your time

Life has a nasty habit of taking up your time with 'stuff to do', and it seems like a constant battle to find time to concentrate on your goals and achieve the things you want. Therefore a vital component in realizing your dreams is time management.

The main thing in managing your time is to prioritize your daily activities. Some stuff is urgent and has to be dealt with now; some is important, but not particularly urgent, so it can be planned into your day or week, or delegated if that is possible for you. When you start prioritizing like this, you will find that a huge amount of 'stuff' you used to spend so much of your time on is neither urgent nor important. You can happily dump it! Think about the worst that could happen if you didn't deal with a lot of it – would it matter a year from now? If not, then it's not a priority. Use Table 4 as a quick reference and start categorizing the 'stuff' that keeps you busy and may be preventing you getting on with achieving the goals, which could take you closer to living your dream.

Table 4

	NOT IMPORTANT	IMPORTANT
NOT URGENT	Dump it	Plan it
URGENT	Delegate it	Do it now

You can use this format in Table 4 to sort out all sorts of 'stuff you do'. Prioritize your social engagements and the appointments you make. Are they really necessary or could you make better use of your time? If you run a business, are you spending time on work you could more usefully delegate? What is causing you stress in your life? Could you rearrange things so that you reduce stress? How about dumping something completely in order to free up some time for the things you would rather be doing? Minimize time spent on things that aren't progressing your goals.

Sometimes we fill our time with unnecessary chores as a way of procrastinating and putting off doing the things we know we need to do. If you think you are doing this, then first of all tackle the things you are putting off first. Take a deep breath and just get stuck in. The rolling friction is easier than the starting friction! In other words, once you start something you've been putting off, it is much easier to keep going.

Another time-management idea is to use lists. Personally, I can't live without my lists! Instead of juggling everything around in your head, try making a master list, then prioritize it, and break it down into manageable bits. You may want to do this on a monthly, weekly or daily basis, whatever suits you best. You may find it helpful to make a list in the evenings ready for the next day. I believe in using your brain for creative thinking, not for storing lists of things you need to do. By writing lists you clear some space in your head for thinking, planning and innovating. When you have your list written down, get the urgent and important stuff out of the way, then make sure you have plenty of time to pursue the goals you have set yourself that help move you towards your dream.

'Time bandits'

Beware of time bandits! These are the people who will happily spend hours chatting to you on the phone or, even worse, who just pop in on you and never know when to go. If you work from home, this can become a real problem. Start screening your calls. Unless the call is urgent, a social chat will wait. You also have to make it clear to people that it is not convenient for them to pop in without warning. You can find a way to get this across without being rude – try not answering the door! Or, simply explain that you need to set certain times aside for work. If you live with other people, make a personal, private space somewhere for yourself, even if it is just a desk in a corner of the bedroom. It is important to have a quiet space to work and think where you will not be disturbed.

'Time bandits' are not always people. Often what we have to do can be organized in a more time-friendly way. For example, we all have to shop for food and other essentials, but don't waste your most productive hours doing tasks like this, which can be done any time, especially these days when you can shop around the clock, or online. Why not leave things like shopping for when you are too tired to tackle your more important tasks? Be aware of your concentration span and your physical limits. It is better to stop and take a break just before you get fed up with an activity. That way, you are more likely to be keen to pick the activity up again later.

Make a list of things you really want to include in your day and put together a timetable that incorporates them. Set aside certain times for each activity or project you are working on, and try to have some sort of routine to your day. Don't be afraid to set alarm clocks to remind you to do something important either. I do this all the time because I tend to get so absorbed in what I'm doing, I lose all track of time. I even have to put sticky notes on the clock to remind myself why I set the alarm! Do whatever it takes to make it happen for you.

9

The power of your subconscious mind

Your subconscious mind is the older, primitive part of your brain, the part that keeps your body's vital functions operating without conscious control. Through complex biofeedback mechanisms, your subconscious controls the delicate physiological mechanisms, and our thoughts alone can alter the most subtle and complex functions of the body. This has huge implications for our ability to change our lives through the power of the mind.

Direct access to your subconscious

Your imagination is the most powerful ally you have when it comes to making dreams come true. What you can imagine, you can create, since everything begins with a thought. Everything around us began with a thought. The everyday things you use, the creative art you see, and the books you read, all began as a thought in someone's mind. You can bring your dream to life in your imagination, and by focusing on it, believing in it, and taking action towards it, you can create it in reality. This is a form of biofeedback called *creative visualization*, and athletes use these techniques to achieve success. They vividly imagine themselves sprinting to the finish line and rehearse the whole race in their mind, step by step. Great golfers practise in their minds – they feel and see themselves hitting the ball with precision. Use your imagination to visualize yourself succeeding and bringing your goals to life.

One method of influencing your subconscious mind is through hypnosis. The word hypnosis is derived from the name of the Greek god of sleep, Hypnos; although hypnosis is similar to sleep, it is actually a state of conscious awareness whereby you are highly open to suggestion. In hetero-hypnosis, another person makes the suggestions, but in self-hypnosis, you make your own suggestions.

Hypnosis has been successfully used as pain control during childbirth and as an anaesthetic during surgery. Hypnosis is probably a function of the right brain since this is concerned with diffuse, intuitive thought. In fact, a group of patients were monitored via

EEGs while having wisdom teeth removed using hypnosis as the only means of anaesthesia. Researchers found that the patients showed more activity in the right side of the brain.

Almost everyone can experience a state of hypnosis and it is a simple and undemanding way of using your brain to influence your body and behaviour. You can literally rewire your brain's neural networks while you relax! We have already discovered that repetition is necessary to create and establish the new neural networks associated with new habits and changes in behaviour, which can lead to substantial life changes. By repeating suggestions while in a highly receptive state of hypnosis, you can effortlessly strengthen your neural networks and bring about a change in behaviour.

Meditation also involves a change in conscious awareness and can influence your subconscious mind when used in conjunction with creative visualization or imagination. Meditation is essentially a process of quietening the mind and focusing on your internal mental imagery while detaching your awareness from the surrounding external environment. This same process is used in hypnosis, and while there may be subtle differences, the effect is the same when suggestions are made to a receptive mind.

Another powerful method is to reach your subconscious directly while you sleep. Although your conscious mind is unaware of your surroundings during sleep, your subconscious is ever vigilant, as we saw when anaesthetized patients were played tapes during surgery. Your altered state of consciousness during sleep can be used to access your subconscious, enabling you to change beliefs and reinforce new neural networks. Your sense of hearing is still highly sensitive during sleep – as you will know if you have ever been awoken by a noise in the night. Even patients in a coma can often still hear, and patients who have recovered have reported conversations they heard while in a coma. Even when someone dies, it is thought that the last sense to disappear is hearing. By playing tapes containing suggestions while you sleep, you are able to access your subconscious mind on a subliminal level – in other words, beneath your conscious awareness.

It seems that by altering our conscious state of awareness through hypnosis, meditation or sleep, we can access our subconscious mind and effectively bring about the changes we are seeking in our lives. We can use this state of receptiveness to affect the physiology of both our brain and body. In particular, we can use it to strengthen the neural networks associated with these changes. By a process of repetition, we can make lasting changes as new neural networks mature and develop. So how can we achieve all this?

Making changes . . . your own reprogramming tapes

An effective way to make repetitious suggestions to your subconscious is by making audiotapes. By making your own tapes, you stay in complete control of the suggestions and can update them as your goals and aspirations develop. All you need is a tape recorder that will record your voice and some audiotapes, along with a script of your suggestions. Once you have made your tape (or tapes), simply play them to yourself while you relax in a hypnotic state, meditate or sleep. Your subconscious mind will do the rest!

Scripts for your tapes ✸

The main points to remember when making tapes are to:

- induce a relaxed state of mind and body;
- elicit changes from this moment on – don't dwell on old behaviour traits that reinforce old neural networks;
- create a new and intense vision of yourself having changed – visual images are extremely powerful;
- repeat your suggestions, goals and action plans to entrench the ideas into new neural pathways.

Try making Mind Maps of the changes you want to make in your life, and work with these to produce a script. Pepper it with suggestions for relaxation and deep breathing, and allow pauses during the script to give yourself time to relax and take those deep breaths in and out. Create intense visual images by describing in detail the 'new you' or the circumstances of your 'new life'. Fill up the whole tape by repeating your script over and over again so that you achieve several repetitions while you relax, meditate or sleep. The idea is to fill your brain with images of your new goals to encourage the creation of new neural networks.

10

Cherish your dream long term

Life will test you every step of the way to see if you are still serious about what you want. The faint-hearted will fall by the wayside at the first hurdle, but when you have a burning desire to make your dreams come true, nothing can stop you from reaching your highest aspirations. Keep breathing, weather the storms, and stay on course. Every goal is a step nearer and you will achieve your dream if you really want it. Remember, it is estimated to take several months to change habits so that new things become second nature to you, so give yourself time to adjust and don't let anyone persuade you to leave 'your path'.

Sometimes it becomes so difficult to keep going that it is tempting to give up. But the enduring sense of achievement and fulfilment from facing and overcoming your challenges is one of the most satisfying human emotions there is. Think of the challenges as part of the journey – a chance to reaffirm your commitment to your plan and an opportunity to learn. Remember that failure is simply the mechanics of success. You have to fail in order to learn, and if you give up every time you fail, you will never achieve anything. Anticipate it and plan for it. Anyone who has ever achieved anything has failed at some point, and often many times over. I have learned my greatest lessons from my biggest mistakes and I know there are more to come.

Coping with setbacks and staying on course

Keep going. When things are tough, find ways to believe in your dream again and find things that inspire you to keep going. Look for inspirational quotes that mean something to you, read the books that resonate with you, and seek out the people who inspire you to stay on track. Sometimes we need to take a break or spend some time getting our balance back when we have been overzealous about achieving our ambitions, but that doesn't mean we have to give up. Take some time out to do different things or simply to 'be', whether it's for an hour, a day, or several weeks, but think of it as part of the plan. You might re-evaluate your goals and improve upon them, but never give up on your dreams. Pace yourself and check that you are managing your time effectively. Sometimes by simply rearranging things or looking again at our priorities, we can find the space to work on our goals. Make some more Mind Maps and subliminal tapes and saturate your brain with your goals and your dreams, and reactivate those neural pathways associated with the changes you want to make.

Don't take it all for granted. Sometimes when we have made some headway and are achieving our goals, we forget what life was like before. Think back occasionally in order to gain a sense of perspective and measure just how far you have come. My life is totally unrecognizable if I think back just 10 or 15 years. It is astounding how much our lives can change when we truly desire something better and work steadfastly towards our dreams.

Most people you meet are concerned with their own lives, and too busy getting themselves tied up in knots worrying about their own problems to worry about what you're up to. When you go home at the end of the day, it is *your* life you have to live, and if you are not happy about the way things are going, then it is only you who can do something about it. When you reach the end of your life it will be you alone who will look back and wish you had followed your heart. You only have yourself to answer to, and you can't blame anyone else if you fail to take control and seek out the things you want out of life.

We all want different things and have a different perspective of the world, so you can't expect others to share your dreams or even to necessarily understand them. Emerson said, 'To be great is to be misunderstood.' Your dreams are special, and until your life changes in ways that people can understand and see, you have to have the courage to do it alone. People don't necessarily have the same vision of the future that you have, since they don't have all the missing pieces of the jigsaw.

People are generally insecure with change and may vehemently resist *your* changes in case it upsets their life as well. Until you have the confidence and momentum to commit to and live your dream, it is probably better to keep it to yourself while you go through the process of finding out what it is you want and putting together an action plan to achieve it. It is too easy to be swayed off your true path in the early stages, so leave other people out of it for now.

You might be worrying about your goals affecting relationships with loved ones and how your plans might change things, since you might be happy about your relationship, but unhappy about your life in other areas. But if someone loves you genuinely for who you are, they can't help but accept you and love you for growing as a human being and wanting to follow your dream. To do otherwise is not real love, but simply clinging on to a false sense of comfort and security for their own benefit, not yours. If you love someone, you want them to be happy and striving to reach their full potential. Are you going to stifle your life and remain trapped so that another person can feel comforted? That is just nonsense. When you have children or other dependants, things are more complicated, of course, but not impossible by any means. It just takes more thought and planning and compromise for everyone concerned. Perhaps you can arrange more help or drop chores that are unimportant in order to create more time. Talk to the significant people in your life and discuss ways you can make it work.

It is wonderful when people accept you as you are and respect your dreams without judgement or prejudice, and without giving unwanted advice, yet you can never hope to please everyone, however hard you try. You are different things to different people: to your children you are a parent; to your special someone you are a partner, husband or wife; to your boss you are an employee. With all these people you will act slightly differently. You can never hope to please everyone, and stay true to yourself. People are generally quite negative, and often it is hard to stay positive and committed to your dream when you are surrounded by negative attitudes. Negative people disrupt your thoughts and your equilibrium. Notice your discomfort around negative people and don't spend time with them. Don't waste time, either, explaining things to people who are controlling, manipulative or obstructive. Refuse to be disrespected and you will gain self-respect. You can choose who you spend time with, so choose to be with people who make you feel good to be alive. Positive supportive people are pleasant and calming to be with. Think of the laws of cause and effect and treat others as you would like to be treated yourself. If you do this, you can't go wrong. Life isn't fair . . . life is simply the way it is. Learn to live without conditions or judgements and be open to the infinite possibilities that surround you.

Enlisting help

Although we can't let others impose their judgements and conditions upon us, we still need other people for the attainment of our goals, both in a practical and a psychological sense. We can tap into the skills, knowledge and wisdom of others in order to fulfil our own purpose. Napoleon Hill calls it the 'Mastermind Alliance', where there is 'co-ordination of knowledge and effort, in a spirit of harmony, between two or more people, for the attainment of a definite purpose'. Mark Victor Hansen and Robert Allen, in their bestselling book *The One Minute Millionaire*, refer to it as the 'Dream Team'. We can achieve extraordinary results when we create a partnership with other like-minded individuals.

Imagine a hospital without the spirit of co-operation and harmony of everyone working for the best interests of its patients. If doctors, nurses, managers, cleaners and a whole host of other personnel, from laboratory technicians and porters to staff from clinics and other departments, did not work with a definiteness of purpose – that is, helping people recover from illness and injury – then the whole place would descend into chaos (and, it could be argued, frequently does!). But imagine the outcome for the patient fighting for his life in an Accident and Emergency department if the doctors and nurses responsible for his care did not work as a team aligned to their purpose.

Likewise, businesses need a group of people working together to achieve their aims; families need cohesion and harmony; couples need synergy and shared values in order to achieve lasting success.

Great teams include partnerships such as Bill Gates and Paul Allen who started Microsoft, and the Wright brothers who built and flew the first aeroplane. The success of a team depends on the alignment of the principles and values of its members, whether it be two people working together or an entire government. Where there is conflict, there is weakness. A team needs to work together as a cohesive whole for otherwise it breaks down. Choose your team carefully. Negative elements and negative people will work against you, not with you. A boat with a hole in its hull is sunk!

Think about your goals and how assembling a 'dream team' would help you to achieve success. Think about your weaknesses and how you could overcome them by working with others. For years I 'failed' to take my business ideas past the early stages. I lacked organization and the heart to follow them through. It was only when I understood myself, accepted my weaknesses and re-evaluated my strengths, that I realized that I was essentially a creative right-brain thinker. I was great at innovating new ideas, but I needed other people with good organizational skills and attention to detail to follow through and take the idea forward into the marketplace. I am essentially an 'ideas' person, and now I concentrate on writing and research, which employs that talent fully. I can also be true to myself, since I know where my weaknesses are and how to compensate for them. I also realized that often you can't do it alone.

Think about the type of help you might need to achieve your goals. Is it practical skills, say a builder, to help build your dream home? A designer to help you plan the interior? Or maybe you need someone to help you find the perfect location to fit in with your personal values? It's likely to be a balance of people with different qualities and attributes, but they will all be aligned to your purpose of building your dream home. Who would you choose to be on your team?

Balancing your dream with others' demands

Although achieving your dreams takes dedication and sustained effort, you also need to balance this with other activities in your life. Balance work with play and rest, and make sure that you take care of your health and well-being. It is stupid to let yourself 'burn out' and end up giving up on your dream. I have been there too, and it is hard to bounce back and find the will to get on track again. You need to pace yourself and take time off now and again to recharge your batteries. Read a book, go for a swim or a good work-out in the gym, and take an evening off now and again. You will find that you come back to your goals with renewed energy and enthusiasm, ready to achieve far more than if you had plodded on tired and jaded. In doing this, you are not taking time off from your dreams – just taking time out to rebalance your life.

Find things that are restorative and relaxing for you physically, mentally and spiritually. Make a list of little things you can do to balance your life in each of these areas. I find a good long walk on the beach or in the countryside is just the thing – physical exercise, a chance to think and plan, and to contemplate the wonders of the universe. Find your own way to de-stress . . . take time out and consider it a priority. Take time to look after your body and mind, and to build the physical and mental strength you need to work towards your dreams.

Success is a journey . . .

As you grow the stakes get bigger. Once you satisfy your goals, you begin to set yourself new challenges. If you don't do this, you become stagnant. Always strive to reach your full potential . . . you will find it is limitless. The only success is in living the life you want. It is not measured by money or material things, only by whether you are growing and developing as a human being. It is not measured by what happens to you, but by how you are dealing with it and learning life's lessons. It is measured by the love you give and the way you treat other people, and everything in the world around you. Be the best person you can be and always follow your dreams. There is no final pinnacle where you can sit and say 'I made it'; there will always be another mountain to climb, another river to cross, and another part of your dream to find. Success is a journey, not a destination. Your 'in tray' will never be empty and you will never know all there is to know. Your amazing, flexible brain will support you all the way once you find the heart to follow your dream . . .

Index